I call you each by name and I say to you,
"It is time to return to Me"

I am the cure for every ill

I am the calm for every storm

I am the comfort for every sorrow

~ Volume Two; Jesus ~

Heavenly Healing

by Bonnie Shoemaker

CMJ
Marian Publishers
and Distributors

Heavenly Healing
By: Bonnie Shoemaker
ISBN: 1-891280-88-0
Library of Congress applied for.
© Copyright 2009: Bonnie Shoemaker

Publisher:

CMJ Marian Publishers and Distributors
PO Box 661
Oak Lawn, Illinois 60454
Telephone: 1-708-636-2995
FAX: 1-708-636-2855
Web Page: www.cmjbooks.com
Email: jwby@aol.com

Permission granted from Direction for Our Times for the use of the messages used throughout the work. Permission granted by the authors of the stories to publish their stories in this work.

Graphics: Pete Massari
              Rockford, IL 61114

Format & Editing:
              Stratum Concepts, Inc
              Oak Lawn, IL 60453
Editorial:
 A very good friend

To my close friend and confidant, Jesus Christ, the Returning King

and

To my precious daughters:

Mallorie Elizabeth (Lewis) Marino

Whitney Lorraine (Lewis) May

and

Taylor Marie Lewis

Table of Contents

Part Five: Returning to the Sacraments

FOREWORD

MY PATH TO JESUS CHRIST THE RETURNING KING

My children, it is during these times when your relationship with Me is of the greatest value.

~Volume One, July 16, 2003, Jesus

I know exactly how many days are left before you appear before Me in the next life. I have special work that needs to be done. Indeed, I have special work for each one of these days remaining to you. If you will say "yes" to Me, I can rest more easily, knowing those tasks will be completed and souls, the certain number attached to your work, will be saved. ~ Volume Two, August 25, 2003, Jesus

Timing is everything. Not our timing, but God's timing. God knows when heaven is needed to resuscitate a soul amidst disabling trials and tribulations. For me, it was two weeks after my father died of cancer. As one of his primary caregivers, I experienced the arduous reality of daily care which challenged me in ways I never expected. At the same time, I dealt with my mother who suffered from bipolar disorder and was in her own state of decline. After Dad's death, a close friend asked if I would be interested in attending a Eucharistic Day of Renewal in Clearwater, FL. She gave me *Volume One* to read to familiarize myself with Anne, a lay apostle. As I read the book on the way to Clearwater, I knew I was being rescued with messages from Jesus Himself. My life drastically changed that day. I gave my "yes" to Jesus to live life as a lay apostle.

Thirteen months later my mother endured a long, difficult death. I survived the emotionally draining roller coaster ride thanks to the *Volumes, Climbing the Mountain* and *Mist of Mercy.* After her death, I decided I wanted to write. I had a few articles published and then I had the idea to interview Anne for a potential article submission. Jesus had other plans for me as a writer. I began hearing other testimonies from lay apostles after joining the local prayer group. Writing an article turned into writing a book of testimonies from around the world illustrating the fruits of this rescue mission.

After *Direction for Our Times* sent the email requesting testimonies for this book, the response was phenomenal. We had given lay apostles a choice of either writing their own stories or receiving a phone call from me for a personal interview. The impact of speaking to so many moved by this mission ignited my heart and moved me to continue seeking more and more lay apostles to enrich my life.

Every person from whom I received testimonies or met in person said the same thing...Jesus was speaking directly to each one, specifically. Whether through the monthly message or *Volumes,* we all hear Him calling us to service. His words comfort, providing guidelines to live our lives and to shine His light to those in darkness. Each situation is unique, and only heaven could touch us individually with words resonating truth so deep in our hearts.

I am forever grateful to all my fellow lay apostles for sharing their personal stories with a complete stranger. But as we all know, once you become a lay apostle, there is an instant connection. For we have been chosen by Our Beautiful Savior to stand together and bring His light to the world through this apostolate.

~Bonnie

PART ONE

A Personal Relationship
With Jesus

Priests and Religious

Priests and religious, holy men and women, console my heart in an extraordinary fashion right now and I am maximizing the tremendous graces I receive from these righteous souls.

~Volume One, July 17, 2003, Blessed Mother

You must view your life through eyes that see as your Savior sees. To clarify, view everything through My eyes. I am Jesus Christ. You are My divine servants. You have been given a share of My divinity through your vocation.

~Volume 4, January 26, 2004, Jesus

Perhaps I was asking too much. But, I wanted to understand why some priests accept the words of Jesus Christ in the *Volumes* and others don't. So, when Fr. Jeff asked what I wanted him to focus on in his testimony, I asked him to answer that question for me. Why did he believe the messages were from heaven? With no expectations of an answer to my question, his following response opened before my eyes...~Bonnie

Fr. Jeff Von Lehmen, KY

Scrutiny for the healing care of the flock!!

I am a diocesan priest from St. Patrick Parish and Shrine in Taylor Mill, KY. It is normal and healthy for a priest to scrutinize over the experiences of mystics and Catholic spiritual movements within the Church. When I scrutinize over something, I do so because I care. I care to see how Christ may or may not be working and returning through His people, His Church. Scrutiny has always been part of our healing and conversion experience. We see in RCIA where converts scrutinize their own lives in order to see and feel more clearly how Christ is wanting to purify, heal, touch and direct them. I think the opposite of scrutiny is indifference. That means I don't care enough to see whether or not something is from Heaven.

In regard to Anne, a lay apostle and the *Volumes*, I was honestly indifferent at first. One summer, at the end of a pilgrimage to Medjugorje, someone in the group handed me a couple of *Volumes* of Anne's. I did not know of Anne at the time (around 2006) or of the *Volumes*. I stuck them in my suitcase as I said to myself, "Yeah, right, another mystic!! What is wrong with the ones we have already?"

Forward a year later. We had just finished a renovation of the parish church. I was asked to help design a stained glass window over the tabernacle facing the sanctuary on one side and an adoration chapel on the other side. The design turned out to be the image of the heart of Christ with drops of mercy flowing from it symbolizing the sacramental life of the Church. The color red stands out and draws one's attention to the tabernacle. Surrounding the heart are the words, "Mir, Mir, Mir" (Peace, Peace, Peace). I was already convinced that strong problems in the human family and human heart, which rob the person and world of inner peace, require a strong Presence if healing is going to be complete.

The Real Presence in Mass and in Adoration is offered as the remedy for hearts along with all the other types of help within the Body of Christ. But I did not know how to connect people with the remedy or to discover a kind of primer to help them begin to desire the Presence again. One day, when this concern was heavy on my mind, I just happened to pull out my suitcase looking for another object. Inside were *Volumes One* and *Two*. *Volume Two* caught my attention perhaps because it is red. The name of the *Volume* is *The Eucharistic Heart of Jesus*. I began to read it. As I read the *Volume*, my indifference was cured that day, and scrutiny began. I started to care about exploring the *Volumes* and apostolate further because in them, there appeared to be God's healing care for His sheep in accord with the Spirit of the Church.

My next step was to get on the internet. Behold, I discovered that Anne had set a time to come to a parish in Louisville, KY. (about two hours from St. Pat's.). I went along with some of our parish staff to participate in that day. You get to know a person by how she prays. I watched Anne pray and intercede for so many of the wounded souls before the Blessed Sacrament. I met Anne, and Fr. Darragh, DFOT Chaplain. I discovered she is completely obedient to her Bishop and also had communication with John Paul II prior to his death. I also found out the connection between Anne and St. Faustina of Divine Mercy.

There was one thing more that happened that day in Louisville. I found myself sitting next to Fr. Damien, who was at that time the Abbot of Gethsamani and now acts as the head guest master for the Trappist monastery (made famous by Thomas Merton) in Bardstown, KY. I leaned over to him asked him what he thought about this whole thing. He said without hesitation, "The *Volumes* got me over the edge." That means that someone as competent in the ways of the human heart and love of God as a Trappist Abbot found, in the writings of Anne, just what the Divine Doctor had ordered. As Providence would have it, the abbot was already booked to come to talk to all the priests of my diocese that following Tuesday for continuing formation of clergy. On Tuesday afternoon, he concluded his remarks by highly recommending for all the priests, *Direction for Our Times* and Anne's *Volumes*. Present were the Bishop

3

and two chancellors. I continue to turn to Fr. Damien for spiritual advice in these matters.

As part of my testimony, I can say that obedience to the Bishop and Church in these matters is the way of the apostolate. The simplest thing I have had to do has been the hardest, TRUST. Never has the Bishop in our diocese openly disapproved of Anne. A bishop is certainly part of the scrutiny process. Personally, I have found that although a bishop cannot give the appearance of approving these kinds of mystical writings, there is still the process the Church has always used by permitting something of possible value to unfold with continuing scrutiny as a sign of care for the flock. Again, scrutiny is the opposite of indifference. I did give Anne's book on *Obedience and the Priesthood* to my Bishop. Again, he demonstrated no outward disapproval. I remain open and obedient to the Bishop myself. Obviously, the *Volumes* themselves encourage that.

Lastly, I want to say one more thing. As I scrutinized the *Volumes* rather than remain indifferent, I found that I also began to scrutinize my own heart. I could add much more about the little ways in which Christ has reordered my life through the *Volumes* so as to become holy for others (which is different than putting on the appearance of becoming holier than others). One quick story should suffice about growth in holiness. I was in San Antonio on retreat with a group of religious for about a week one summer. Each day, I would go to a nearby parish church named St. Peter's. I would sit in a little Blessed Sacrament chapel for about 1 or 2 hours a day just reading the *Volumes* and the Scriptures. I noticed that the tabernacle was sitting literally on a huge rock. I could not help but to think of the words of Jesus to St. Peter, "And so I say to you, you are Peter, and upon this rock I will build my church, and the gates of the netherworld shall not prevail against it."*Matt. 16:18.* I thought of something Anne had said: Picture all of us in the Catholic Church on the same side of the rock pushing in the same direction. Now don't misunderstand what I am about to say. I was never a rebellious or defiant priest. I didn't promote abortion or any lack of truth. However, I did have deep within my subconscious a feeling of alienation from Church authority, a feeling of being targeted and looked down upon but never supported. I even at one time imagined Cardinal Ratzinger to be a restrictive, cold, calculating intellect.

The *Volumes* have helped me to heal this hidden bitterness or resentment. I began to change my subconscious view of church authority. I knew there were so many problems in the world, so much hurt and pain that needed healing. I got down on my knees and prayed deeply for the Pope and church leaders in front of the Blessed Sacrament. I wanted at a deeper level to work with them possible; to push that big rock in unity with them. Only that way, could we speed up Christ's healing in the world. I am developing this unity in my own life.

Now, for example, instead of reading what others say about the Pope through the press which often is slanted one way or another, I simply read his writings directly. I can see such a difference from what he says and what others may say he is saying. All of this is to say that since I have moved from indifference to scrutiny of the *Volumes*, I myself am being directed to scrutinize my own heart. Scrutiny is definitely for the care of the flock.

> *You have been given a share of My divinity through your vocation. In this way, it is not you who leads sheep back to the fold, but Me who leads through you.*
> ~Volume Four, January 26, 2004, Jesus

The Dallas lay apostle prayer group welcomed me with open arms. The love, support and commitment to this rescue mission and each other beamed from each beautiful face. One of those faces was Fr. Joseph Mary, a young friar with genuine love for Our Lady and Her Son.

I wanted to snatch Father right from this group and bring him back to Florida with me... ~Bonnie

Fr. Joseph Mary Deane, TX

I am a member of the Franciscan Friars of the Renewal, the CFR's at the Dallas lay apostles prayer group currently stationed at Sacred Heart in Ft. Worth, Texas.

I had a friend from Ireland who mentioned there was a movement there and asked if I wanted the books to read. He said they could send them to me for free, so I said sure. I thought, it's free, I'll check it out. And at the right time, they did. Months had gone by and I completely forgot about them (the *Volumes*). I was on a retreat, a silent contemplative retreat, and as I was leaving, one of the images they gave me was little parachutes, little packages coming down from heaven. Jesus was going to be sending me little presents from heaven at this time in my life. I had no idea what that meant. I liked the image, but I had no idea. I got home, already forgetting about the image. As I came into my room at the Friary, I opened the door and there was a box sitting on my floor. I had no idea what it was. I opened the box and there were all these books inside. I was thinking, what are all these books in my room? I heard the voice of Jesus saying, "these are the presents I was sending you from heaven." My initial reaction when seeing a box of books as a priest and religious - you get so many books and devotions, so many different things - you have to read this Father, you have to read that Father...If I read everything I received I would never have time to be a priest! So, honestly, I usually don't. Then again, the voice inside of me - the Holy Spirit - said to just pick up and read. These were the presents He was sending me from heaven.

I picked up the first one *(Volume One)*, curious about what they were and within a couple of pages, I knew they were for me. They were a direct, real message from heaven for me at that time. I was hearing Jesus a lot on the retreat in the silence speaking very clearly. When I got back, I was expecting that to continue. But instead, He put me into a desert time. But one of the ways I knew He was going to continue to speak to me was through the *Volumes*. He was going to speak to my heart through them. It would be more a matter of trust. I wasn't going to hear Him in my heart all the time. I was reading the *Volumes* regularly, and something would come to my heart in prayer. A thought would come and I would question, is this from the Lord? Is this something you are asking of me, Lord? Is this Your will? Every time I would pick up the *Volumes* or pick up the book I was reading, it would be a complete confirmation of what I felt the Lord was putting in my heart, complete and total confirmation. Time and time again, this would enliven my preaching, especially climbing the mountain of holiness, seeking God's will in the ordinary things of life, for myself, working with people and priests as well as creating images of heaven and of purgatory.

The messages are so beautiful. I have consecrated my devotion completely to Our Lady. I see her as my mystical spouse in the same way nuns see Jesus (as brides of Christ). Reading the parts about Our Lady in *Mist of Mercy* (purgatory book). I can't read those parts without crying because they are so beautiful (Our Lady's intercession). So, in sharing this with people who are afraid of purgatory, or don't understand purgatory, and those who don't see heaven as something that's worth striving for, or even believe in heaven will help them in time.

When I was reading the books, I wasn't reading them as books, but as prayers. Jesus was speaking to my heart. I would read a little bit each day and allow it to soak in and meditate. That would be my food for the day. Again, it was always a confirmation that whatever the Lord would speak to me in my heart the day before, the next morning I would read something from the *Volumes* during the mediation hour. This has been a tremendous help to me personally in my own spiritual growth,

7

helping me to understand the world better: sin, holiness, heaven, purgatory, hell...everything.

Allowing this to be a part of my priesthood through youth retreats – I take the book *Heaven Speaks to Young Adults* – and read certain quotes during my talks. I typically begin by saying, "I want to read a letter to you from Jesus for young adults and what Jesus is asking of you." If people come and ask me where it's from, I tell them. I finish a talk by saying it's Jesus' personal message for young people here, everywhere, in Kentucky, Ohio, Florida, about living holiness. I allow Him to pick the passages. There are some I prefer, but sometimes He'll put something else in my heart. I am encouraging everyone I can – I've given the *Volumes* and other literature to family members and friends.

I was talking to a friend of mine who is a National Dominican. She asked me what I had been doing and I told her about *Direction for Our Times*, and since I mentioned it several other times during our conversation, she said, well, you've said it three times, so I think I'm supposed to get those and read them. And I said, "Yeah, you definitely need to!" A number of the friars have them and read them as well. They've been profoundly moved by them, too. I use the *Volumes* to increase my personal holiness and to support the priesthood, religious vocations, and especially the people.

When I give a talk on the Eucharist at a parish I'll take a quote from the *Eucharistic Heart of Jesus* because people will say, "Oh, it's such a beautiful quote!" Even in our lay associates group I was looking for a prayer for them to say every day and I thought, I'll get the card with the Allegiance prayer and Morning Offering on it. It's not a lay apostle prayer group, but I couldn't find a better prayer to use, so I use this one. And, it has the *DFOT* information on it so they can look into there as well.

I am no longer walking your earth in the physical sense. I do not need to, because I have you to do that for Me.
~Volume Four, January 26, 2004, Jesus

Fr. Mike Snyder, Picayune, MS

I am a Catholic priest in Picayune, MS, a small town north of New Orleans, LA, USA. I have visited the local county jail a number of times, offering the sacrament of confession each time. Last month, a lay minister organized a visit after receiving his prison ministry training. His first visit revealed a dozen Catholics. He gave them the book, *Heaven Speaks to Prisoners*. The next week he lined up a dozen confessions. While I was there, I asked what inspired them to make a confession. They said it was the little booklet, *Heaven Speaks to Prisoners*. Thank you for this wonderful little jewel that moved these men with hardened hearts to a humble visit with Jesus in confession. They all wanted to receive Holy Communion and did afterwards. Praise Jesus.

I see so many in need of Me, and truly, they shall have Me. Bring My words to those who suffer. My words will be the balm you will use to nurse souls back to wellness.
~Volume Two, August 22, 2003, Jesus

Father Bill McCarthy, CT

I learned about *Direction for Our Times* through Focus Ministry. When I recorded some programs on a personal relationship with Jesus, Char Vance, Mary Lou McCall and Janie Harney were so excited about a visionary from Ireland, Anne, a mother of six children. They said I had to read some of the messages and handed me *Volume Two*. They were so enthralled with it. They said the messages were so simple, so powerful that they must be from heaven. I talked to Archbishop

9

Hannan who was enthralled with the book also. He had done a program on the messages of *Volume Two*.

Every Thursday I, along with others, give a teaching on four of the messages. We have been doing that for some months now. We have already finished *Volume One*. We get between 80 and 100 people every Thursday to read the messages. The more we read them, the more we realize how simple and powerful and personal they are. What these messages teach everyone is that God speaks to all of us simply, lovingly, powerfully and practically. The messages about God's presence among us show us: the necessity of listening to Him and to His Will; that we're not alone; the powerfulness of Truth; and that giving Him thanks really does heal worry and fear. Trusting and hoping in Him really does heal depression. His love really does heal loneliness and rejection. Forgiveness does heal bitterness and hatred on one hand but also the guilt.

The Eucharist is a healing sacrament and the power of the Holy Spirit is present in our bishop and every person. Every Christian who reads the messages develops a more personal relationship with Jesus, especially in His Sacred Heart, and through His Mother. All become more loving and forgiving as they accept the mission of giving time and space to work with Jesus. The messages are so powerful not only because of the affirmations, but because of the witness of so many lay people who say their lives have been so deeply touched by these messages. So I firmly believe in them, and I promote *DFOT*. I've always said my sheep hear my voice and Anne is certain proof of that. Every anti-Christian should be able to listen to God speak from without, also from within.

When we sit in Eucharistic Adoration or Mass, we open ourselves up to the "three flows of the Spirit" that Anne speaks of. The flow of God's insights bubble up into our minds – that prophetic love; that from God's love is a love that flows in to our hearts and with His power then flows into our lives which becomes the light that flows into a darkened world.

If you are viewing your priesthood from My eyes, you will become accustomed to seeing the vast view. Your every priestly act impacts eternity because your every priestly act impacts souls in one way or another.
~Volume Four, January 28, 2004, Jesus

Peter

I first came across *Direction for Our Times* on the website 'Our Lady of All Peoples' during my Novitiate in 2007. I am a religious missionary preparing for the priesthood. The thing that I found most touching about the messages was that one gets a very strong sense of Christ's humanity and how both chronological time and eternity are more closely interwoven than we often think. *Conversations with Our Eucharistic Lord* is the one *Volume* I return to most frequently. It fills my heart with much consolation just thinking about all the love and graces that Jesus wants to give us and those for whom we pray if we just ask Him.

You must spend time alone with Me so that We can be certain that this gift is being used to its fullest advantage in your soul. I wish to do this for you, My beloved servant.
~Volume Four, January 29, 2004, Jesus

Sr. Elizabeth Tuttle, PBVM, England

I am a Presentation Sister living in England, having recently celebrated the Diamond Jubilee of my Religious Profession. Looking back over the years I have much to thank the Lord for, but especially the graces and blessings of the last three and a half years when I first became acquainted and involved with the lay apostolate of Jesus Christ the Returning King.

At that time, August 2005, I felt Our Lady was prompting me to spend a week in Knock at her Shrine there. About half way through the week I met an old friend, Sr. de Sales Egan, a Presentation Sister like myself. Over a chat she pulled out a few of the *Volumes* from her bag. Handing them to me she said: "I prayed this morning the Lord would show me to whom to give these books; they are for you."

How little did I realize at the time that I was becoming the recipient of such spiritual treasures and how subsequently all of Anne's books published by *Direction For Our Times* would become such a source of spiritual reading, nourishment and encouragement.

When I was first handed the *Volumes*, I accepted them somewhat cautiously, being skeptical about private revelation. However, as I read them and began to share extracts from them with friends, I became convinced of their authenticity, especially as these friends felt the Lord was speaking to them as they listened. Soon I found myself being requested to obtain the *Volumes* and since at that time I wasn't aware of anybody stocking the books in England, I found out how Catherine and Victor Spillane had the responsibility of disseminating the books on behalf of *DFOT* in Ireland. Having made that discovery I kept them busy and they kept me informed of developments.

About that time when I first heard about Anne, a lay apostle, and her mission, I was invited to lead a weekend retreat for the Zion Community Associates near London. The theme they had chosen was "The Second Coming!" Very soon after that I was asked if I could possibly lead a day of Renewal for a Christian group on the Wirral, near Liverpool, as the appointed speaker for the day was unable to fulfill his commitment. When I was informed that their theme for the day was "The Second Coming," I knew I couldn't refuse, because I believe the Lord was involved in all this.

Soon I was to receive a confirmation that I was being called to spread the Mission of the Apostolate of Jesus Christ the Returning King in England. While making my own personal retreat I was prayed with by a very gifted person to whom the Lord seemed to give the following words for me: "My beloved child, I am using you in the weaving of the fabric of My Second Coming. You will help choose the threads to interweave the structure that will be so strong and reach into eternity." I was deeply moved by these words and felt I was being anointed for this special Mission.

In no time doors started opening. For example, I was invited to speak on the lay apostolate during workshops at the Catholic Charismatic Conference in Birmingham for three consecutive years, at the New Dawn Conference in Walsingham over the last two years, at a Liverpool Prayer Group meeting attended by about 80 people, in Medjugorje to a group of English pilgrims on two occasions, just to mention some. Of course, I encouraged my listeners to become lay apostles and to start monthly prayer groups, something I myself had done in my own parish. How blessed and privileged this servant of the Lord has been in being instrumental to some extent at least in spreading His Mission in England.

Recently, we've had our first Eucharistic Day of Renewal in this country, which was well attended and greatly blessed under the leadership of Anne, and *DFOT* Chaplain, Fr. Darragh Connolly. We pray it is the first of many more to come!

> *Truly, the humility of My chosen souls softens My heart and deflects punishment from a cold world, undeserving of the mercy of its God.*
> ~Volume Two, August 29, 2003, Jesus

> *But you house My Spirit. And they will see Me in you and through your vocations and service to Me.*
> ~Volume Four, February 2, 2004, Jesus

You are an asset to the Kingdom of your
Father. I intend to make the most possible
use of your commitment to Me if you will
allow Me.
~Volume Four, February 2, 2004, God the Father

Discerning a vocation to the priesthood or religious life requires not only good listening skills to hear God's voice in your heart, but strength...real strength. Making the choice to live your life for God, shepherding His children and abandoning the worldly view requires commitment that very few possess. I grew up in a household where priests were family friends who visited our house quite often. But I have never known a young person at the beginning of this journey. Meeting the "Bailieborough Seven" as they are lovingly called, changed my life more than they will ever know. They are young men and women, the ages of my own daughters, loving Christ so much they would do anything for Him. Whether they discern they are called to religious life or not, they have made me a better person and a better parent. Their love of Christ is infectious and make being Catholic very cool... I am blessed to call them friends.

Keith W. Ireland, Discerning a vocation to the Priesthood

My name is Keith and I am twenty-three years old. I grew up in a good Catholic family. Despite that, by the time I was sixteen I wasn't going to Confession. I remember how scared I was thinking the priest would yell at me (even though he never did). I barely paid attention in Mass. I kept thinking I'd heard this a thousand times before and they never say anything new. This was the same for every sacrament. I had an excuse for everything! I became progressively worse in the years to come. I replaced God with whatever I wanted. I started doing drugs because people who did drugs agreed with me that there was no point in going to church. I started drinking because that's what I thought real "men" did. Because I wanted to be viewed as a man I ran around any girl I could find. As the saying goes "misery loves company."

I met a girl in November of 2005. She was the first woman I took seriously. I can honestly say I fell head over heels in love with her at first sight. We started dating, and I knew something had to change. So, I quit doing drugs, I cut way down on drinking and for the first time I only had eyes for one girl. Her family went to Mass every Sunday, so I started going with them. I found myself hearing the same words at Mass but I found new meaning in them. The more I heard, the more peace I felt. In the next year we got engaged.

One day my Mom handed me a stack of books and asked me to read them. She kept referring to them as "the *Volumes*." I remember thinking 'why don't they have a name, why so mysterious?' I put them on my bookshelf and there they sat for a year or so.

In 2007 I came down with a severe case of chicken pox. I was bed-ridden for two weeks. Those two weeks changed my life forever. While lying down one day, I reached for the remote to the TV, and it wasn't there. There was a red book sitting there in its place. I picked it up I looked at the front and it was *Volume Two*. I flipped it over to read the back cover. I was blown away! I knew Jesus at that moment. I knew where I was getting it wrong. The strange part was, all I felt was pure love and acceptance. By now my girlfriend had agreed to marry me, so I told my fiancée about these feelings, and she looked at me like I was crazy. She wanted nothing to do with the books. I didn't push in anyway so if she wanted to read them it would be for her not for me.

Through my friend Rob, I was invited to help Nora McCarthy with a Recharge event in Kentucky a year later. Just before we started I slipped into the Adoration Chapel for a quick prayer. I knelt down and looked at Jesus. In my heart I knew I was being called to the priesthood. There was no question about it. He asked, and in my heart, I said yes. But at the same time, I thought to myself, I have a fiancée. I can't just leave her. My heart was torn in two. I kept all this to myself and continued on with the weekend.

When I got home I knew what I had to do. I prayed a lot that week! I didn't know what to say to my fiancée. So I went to her house and started to talk. It was the hardest thing I've ever done. To this day, I'm not sure what I said. It was like an out of body experience. I believe Jesus took over for those moments. I hated myself for doing that to her, but at the same time it had to be done.

As I got into my car to leave I asked God, 'what should I do now?' After a week my mom was in contact with *Direction for Our Times,* and Anne, had been asked to start two discernment houses. Anne and Father Darragh invited me to be a part of the discernment community for a year. So needless to say I packed my bags! I took the chance and ran with it. The Lord opened the door and I ran through. So on the 1st of October 2008 the "Servants of the Returning King" community was born.

I've come to a final decision that I am called to the priesthood and I will keep on discerning that through my time in the seminary. My vocation has been given all it needs to grow here. I will always be grateful to Jesus for these words that Anne has recorded. Please pray for me and all lay apostles.

Young men of this troubled world, search your soul. You will find Me there and perhaps you have been created to lead in this time of transition. You need fear nothing because your Jesus will see to all. I am your beginning and your end.
~Volume Four, February 2, 2004, Jesus

Emma McDermott, age 23, County Cavan, Ireland, (Discerning)

So, how did I become involved in the mission? It's kind of blurry for me. I was living a completely worldly life in college dealing with the usual priorities – drinking, boys, going out, and clothes. I forgot about my family. My new friends and social group became more important to me. I only realized how important my family was to me after moving home from college. They were the only people who knew the 'real' me. I wasn't myself. I felt depressed. I had a boyfriend but we were not happy together.

The day the turning point in life came, I was driving along with my mother. She had just come back to the faith. She always went to Mass but only went through the motions. Now she was starting to 'get God.'

We were driving along in the car, probably going on another shopping trip where I was trying to spend as much money as possible on things I felt would fill the void for a few hours or even a few minutes.

I was staring out the window on the long journey with my mother, and said, "There has to be more to life than this, clothes, boyfriends, friends, and drinking." I was really angry. So my mother turned to me and said: "There is more Emma! Don't you know what it is?" I sat up and said "Ohhhhh, really?!?" I was expecting a real answer as the solution to my problems. She said "It's God, Emma." I am ashamed of this now, but I just shook my head and said "Oh, please." I fell back down into my state of depression. However, she had planted a seed. It played on my mind. I knew my mother was a lot happier than she used to be. I wondered if it was because I had come back to the family after ignoring them for the last couple of years.

Then she gave me a spiritual book. I read a couple chapters and couldn't get very far. I kept going out drinking and still trying to fill that void. But, God was planting little seeds in me that I didn't know about. When I look back, I can see it now.

Then I read, *Climbing the Mountain*. I was very slow to understand but all this time there was a change in me. Actually, I didn't know who I really was. I thought I was the girl who went out and partied all the time. I was only interested in myself and my wants. Only now am I finding who I really am. All that time I was searching. After reading CTM, there was a tugging in my heart that just wouldn't leave me alone.

I started going to Adoration and saying the Rosary. Our Lady was interceding in my life. Different little things were happening giving me the courage I hadn't had before. My mother brought me for prayer to a man. He prayed with me. I must have cried for almost an hour. It was healing. I didn't know it at the time. I thought, "What is this?" The tears were just flowing. He told me Our Lady was very close to me. He told me things that, my mother, my family and friends at the time were probably afraid to say to me.

I was bitter and angry. I was afraid to acknowledge these things to myself at the time. There were things that needed to be changed. I had to face them if I wanted to give myself completely to God. At the time, I could have burst out crying or laughing. These changes seemed impossible. How do you undo everything you've done since you were a teenager?

Then I discovered confession. It really helped me. Through confession God gave me the strength to start making the changes. It had begun. From this point, my faith grew. I started reading V*olume Two* and then moved on to the *Mist of Mercy*. As I read, I had a profound personal experience of God's love for me. Although my faith was growing, it felt like I was taking a step forward in faith and three steps back. I was dancing around and not giving myself completely. I was saying, "Well, God, now I'll go to Mass. I'll go to Adoration. I'm developing a relationship with You, but don't ask me to give anything up." I was living a worldly life and trying to serve God at the same time.

Through reading the book *Serving in Clarity*, I received the grace to realize that if I was going to serve God, it had to be complete. That was and is still something I continue to struggle with.

Soon after this I began going to the Lay Apostle Prayer Group in my local town, Bailieborough, County Cavan, on the first Thursday of every month. I loved going and never missed it. Anne, a lay apostle speaks at this prayer group every month. There was Adoration and confession available. I received so many blessings.

In August, I was preparing to go to the prayer group and on the way thought I had enough time to drop in to my friend's house. After visiting I came out to start my car. It wouldn't start. This was the first time I missed out on the prayer group and ended up staying at my friend's house that night. It was very disappointing.

The next day I went home and my mother told me about what had happened at the prayer meeting the night before. Two discernment communities had been set up by *Direction for Our Times*. The young men and women in the discernment communities were introduced to everyone. There were young women in one house and young men in another.

Hearing this was like a dream come true for me. I felt God calling me to work in the mission. I didn't know what this could involve. I had only worked with young children. So I said: "God, I have no talents in that area."

At the next first Thursday prayer meeting, I had the chance to meet all the young people who had entered community. I couldn't believe we had so much in common and could talk openly about the faith and our experiences with the *Volumes*. I had been in a social group where the name of Jesus was only used as a curse word. I had not had anyone my own age to talk with about God. It was such a blessing for me to meet them.

I prayed for a couple of months to discern if God wanted me to quit my teaching job half way through the year and enter community. I knew I would have to trust God completely in this and so I prayed: "if You really want me to do this God, you'll find a replacement for me."

I felt called to work with the apostolate, but couldn't really imagine it happening. I was thinking, "Emma you're giving up your job and money?" There had to be another way around it. Did God really want me to give up my job and work for the mission? Or, did He want me keep my job and work for the apostolate in my spare time? What exactly was He calling me to do?

I was leaving Mass on a Friday evening and thought perhaps I would talk to Anne to get some clarity. However, this seemed impossible because she was always tied up with somebody. I walked out of the church and Anne was talking to someone. So, I turned and walked towards my car. Suddenly, on my left was Anne walking beside me all alone.

I said, "Hello Anne." I'm sure she knew my face from being friends with the guys in community but it was quite dark so I introduced myself and said, "It's Emma." She said, "Oh hey Emma." She started talking and seemed to ask me all the right questions that God knew I had been waiting to be asked. We discussed that I had been discerning entering community. She said: "what does your heart tell you?" Even though it is so simple, no one had asked me before and I didn't need to answer it. I felt a deep peace and certainty in my soul. I feel like I didn't decide with my mind, Jesus put the answer in my heart. It was within me. Because I am such an indecisive person, I decided I could never decide! So Jesus must have put it in my heart.

After the conversation with Anne, I went for a coffee with my mother and said, "Well, I'm entering community." I hadn't even asked Anne yet, but something in me just knew. Then I told the guys in community and they were not at all surprised.

Before this I had gone on a retreat with the Recharge team and loved it.

I am now in my first month of community life and in this year will try to discern my vocation.

> *Heed My words and take My hand and I will put you on the path I have laid out for you. It will feel right to you as it has been designed only for you by your God, who knows you with a perfect and complete knowledge.*
>
> ~Volume Two, August 29, 2003, Jesus

Karen Anne, Ireland

A few years ago, I remember going for a walk. I remember feeling content. Various struggles I had as a teenager and early 20's were no longer there. I'd finally graduated from college, had a good job, good career, great friends who loved me and I was no longer drinking. I remember kind of thinking... ticking all this off in my head but realizing I had a hollow feeling inside. I remember putting this aside- I presumed this hole would be filled if I met a man.

Anyway, I didn't labor thinking of this... life went on. I knew I wanted to change myself and my lifestyle. I started going back to Mass occasionally. Not because I believed, but because I felt this was a "good" thing to do. After a few months, I heard Anne's testimony. When I heard of Heaven, Purgatory and this mission, I was captivated. I remember feeling so joyful. How did I forget this? God was real, and He loved me! That was so amazing. I was nearly amused that I'd forgotten this. The reality of God's presence with me became apparent. I started to read the *Volumes*, and it was such a joyful experience. Jesus was real! I was full of joy discovering Him. I started to go to Mass a lot more regularly, adoration and confessions. I remember being at the photocopier at work and wondering why I was so happy. I realized I had a "falling in love" feeling. Then I realized that I was! I was falling in love with Jesus.

A few months later I was traveling. I was on my own and I got involved in volunteer work for selfish reasons. I wanted to make friends. But when I met those women on the streets, truly my heart was opened. And I felt such great love for them. Some were angry but I understood, I would have been angry too. Some were in so much pain. I knew they could have been me as our stories were the same. The women taught me so much about God. I saw how God loved them in their pain, in their addictions and they were not alone in the abuse they suffered. I felt at home in the drug fueled streets with them. It was most bizarre. I felt Jesus on these streets.

For the first time in my life I realized I didn't have this vacuum like I used to. While traveling, I'd become close to a friend. He was a good man and was everything I wanted. We had fun, laughed together, were honest with each other and he was cute! I was attracted to him. I knew we were getting closer, but there was something holding me back. Religious life was attractive to me for a while, but I ignored it as a daydream or escapism. I loved these women, I loved the Church, and I loved my faith. I loved the confidence God gave me in life. He gave me Hope for these women. Hope for me. I did think about going back to college to be a nurse or social care as I so desperately wanted to help these women. But I knew this wasn't it either. It wasn't enough. I'm now in community for one year to discern where it is God is calling me. I don't know if it will be as a sister or a mother, but with both options, I am left filled with hope.

Such will be Our union that you will consult Me on everything. Your life will reflect heaven. Souls will be drawn to you because of this and you will be equal to the representation of your God.

~Volume Two, September 1, 2003, Jesus

Women

Women of the world, rejoice. Your salvation is at hand. Your children's children will be joyful followers of the light.
~Volume Four, January 9, 2004, Jesus

The heart is known as the source of love and the receptacle of love, so I, Jesus, tell you that I want to possess your heart. When it is all simplified, as it should be, I am saying that I want you to love Me. I love you.
~Heaven Speaks to Those Who Don't Know Jesus,
December 21, 2006, Jesus

Women tend to be pleasers...caregivers. We focus intently on our marriages and/or relationships, our children, and just about anything else our minds can imagine. Stabilizing ourselves and our immediate surroundings in a world spinning out of control is a heavy cross to carry, especially when we try to do it alone, without God. We feel like failures when our children make poor choices; when our significant other leaves; or when we are faced with seemingly impossible tasks. Scripture tells us, "I alone know the plans I have for you, plans to bring you prosperity and not disaster, plans to bring about the future you hope for. Then, you will call to me. You will come and pray to me, and I will answer you." *(Jeremiah 29: 11-12)* Why is it so hard to trust God with our lives? To take situations where we feel like failures and turn them into blessings knowing God changed our course to avoid disaster? I have learned from Anne's messages that the more I sit back and look at the big picture, accepting outcomes I didn't anticipate, the more my life peacefully flows... ~Bonnie

Joyce M., Fort Myers, FL

My world had just been turned upside down. Fate, it seemed, delivered a blow with immediate, sobering impact; a blow that still affects my life today. I was about to experience the absolute worst 24 hours of my life. The only way to keep my sanity, minute by minute, was with the constant recital of two blessed prayers to Mary; the Hail Mary and Memorare. I must have prayed them both a thousand times.

It all began with a phone call. My 84 year old mother, afflicted with Alzheimer's, just lost her husband of 23 years. "Joe" was 15 years younger than mom and as her disease progressed, he had literally blossomed into a patient and understanding caregiver. He was a simple, uneducated man whom we all took for granted at times as a stepfather. However, as my mom's disease progressed, a husband's love morphed into something deeper and more compassionate. He thrived on caring for her, and all the family was at peace knowing Mom was safe and loved; we all went on with our lives. Then that phone call came. A heart condition took him early and unexpectedly! Mom was alone. My husband and I had agreed to take care of her many years prior should anything happen to Joe. Without warning, that time had come. We immediately made arrangements to fly to mom's home in Arkansas. The family decided it was best for me, her daughter, to break the news about the death of her husband. We arrived to find a frightened, confused woman. I was still trying to figure out, with less than 24 hours' notice, how to break this awful news to my mother. Given her Alzheimer's, I would have to break this news to her over and over again. Plus, I had to convince her she was to come live with my husband and me in Florida, too much to consider even for a coherent thinker under such circumstances. My two brothers and family arrived soon thereafter, and in a whirlwind six days, Joe was buried, her personal belongings packed up, legal papers filed, dogs adopted, rental vehicle procured, U-Haul trailer packed to bursting and everyone trying to convince mom it was time to leave for her new home several states away in Florida. She was having none of it and was convinced she could live alone for a few months until she sorted through her belongings. She had no idea she was totally incapable of caring for herself.

How do you get an 84 year old mother, in complete disagreement with moving anytime soon, let alone "right now" into a rented SUV hauling a U-Haul trailer? Misdirection was the plan. One brother took her to visit her sister a few homes away while the rest of us ran around in a flurry of activity doing a final packing and shoving last minute items for my mom in a suitcase. We were not nearly anywhere complete in our packing when we received an urgent call from my aunt: "If someone doesn't come and get her right now, she's insisting she is going to walk back home!" Everything stopped and my husband and I drove off to "pick up" my mom. Mom, of course was anticipating a three minute drive, not a 22 hour marathon. I leave to your imagination the conversations, words, feelings and emotions exchanged while all cooped up in a packed SUV for 22 hours.

Coincidentally, this same weekend Anne, a lay apostle, was in Illinois. I had so wanted to attend her retreat with my dear friend Bonnie who was scheduled to interview her for an article. Ever since we both attended Anne's retreat a few years prior in Clearwater with our husbands, Bonnie had clearly experienced a spiritual awakening with her faith growing stronger ever since. I could physically see the transformation in her life. She was so exuberant about having a personal meeting with Anne; Bonnie's enthusiasm was electric. My thoughts were of her, Anne and my "Memorare's" when Bonnie called my cell phone about six hours into our return road trip. She was bursting at the seams with joy from her experience with Anne. All I could say through choked backed tears and voice was "pray for us." I had never needed prayers more in my life.

Twenty-two straight hours on the road and we were finally home. Thank God! Mom was sleeping in her new bedroom, my exhausted husband and I tending to household necessities after being gone for a week when Bonnie called and asked if she could stop by. She brought a care package of food, a warm loaf of her husband's homemade bread, and a new book of Anne's, *Serving in Clarity,* she had picked up at the retreat.

That evening as I lay on the family room sofa just outside of mom's room so I could be close by in case she awoke, I decided to open the book Bonnie had gifted me as I needed my God and Comforter more than ever. The first words I read were:

> ***Be at peace in the sufferings that I send. My apostles in this time will carry crosses with Me, in all resignation. Through your docile acceptance of the cross, I will draw two things. One, I will make you a saint. Two, I will flow rich and constant graces through you into the world.***
>
> ~Serving in Clarity, January 1, 2007, Jesus

That was all I needed to stop my excruciating heartache and to begin experiencing peace. He was talking directly to me!

Thank you, God! Thank you, Lord Jesus! Thank you, Mary! Thank you, Anne! And thank you my dear, accepting, loving husband.

Note: My dear friend Joyce's mother is now 86 years old and being cared for by her loving daughter and son-in-law in their home. Although her Alzheimer's has progressed, Mom's sense of humor has not waned. I know those moments are precious and few, but when they happen, the joy in my friend's eyes is Christ's love radiating into my heart.

I look into the world at this time and there is darkness, it is true, but there is also light and that light comes from your commitment to Me. The angels see your service and they rejoice. The saints see your service and they applaud. Our mother, Mary, sees your service and she is comforted. I, Jesus Christ, see your service and I experience delight. You are part of a team, My team.

~Serving in Clarity, January 1, 2007, Jesus

The Dallas lay apostle prayer group with whom I was blessed to visit, welcomed me with open arms. There is something about being surrounded by lay apostles that is familial. Nobody is a stranger. We all have the same goal - to follow Jesus Christ and shine His light to those in darkness while in our exile on earth. ~Bonnie

Eleanor W., Dallas, TX

It was with great reluctance that I finally decided to read the *Volumes.* While they were recommended by a trusted source, it seems to me there are more messengers and messages today than anyone needs. To discern and then embrace these mystical matters is a serious task.

I chose to begin with *Volume Nine,* on Angels. After reading the first three messages in that little *Volume,* I was amazed that I felt in my heart God was speaking directly to me. I was keenly aware from these writings of God's love, compassion, mercy and direction for me personally. I had to admit, God was again issuing a beautiful invitation to His beloved souls to respond to His love for them. Like for so many, they continue to be for me a source of hope and encouragement time after time as they are reread over and over.

It is not a stumbling block for me to believe that in this Age of Disobedience God has initiated a Rescue Mission for souls in which He will send His Son as Our Returning King. With God being the seat of love, it seems only natural He would choose to use the love of lay apostles to help accomplish His mission. May we all follow His direction.

> *I speak today to all mothers. You are living in a time when mothers are no longer honored for the important role they play in the protection and development of society. Mothers, you are the cornerstone of the home and the home is the place where a person's soul begins his or her critical formation.*
> ~Volume Six, June 7, 2004, Mary (an unknown saint)
> Speaks to Mothers

Holly K., IN

Through the books, I feel like I have a friendship with Him. I thought I did before. I always had Him on my mind and carried Him around with me. I just learned a lot from the books. I didn't realize there were things I could do to make a difference. I didn't understand how important prayer time was. I would always feel myself slipping away before. Now I realize He's telling us not to be haphazard about it. I have to make the initiative to uphold that part of the friendship and let Him do the work. But, I didn't understand that we have to accept His invitation to us. He can't come in until we invite Him. And I didn't realize how much He and heaven need our prayers. I just think this is awesome!

When I got the *Volumes*, the first one I read was *Volume Six,* the one on families. Shortly before I received it in the mail, I was in desperate need of encouragement for being a stay at home mom. Everybody I know has to work. I have been very blessed that I don't have to worry about that right now. Other than my sister, I don't have anyone to talk to about it. It seems I'm in a whole different world than everybody else. I almost felt I was looked down upon for not having a career. I did go to college, but it seems like most people ask where I went to school and why I'm not working. I felt like being home with my children caused others to look down on me. I felt undervalued, even insecure, although I knew I shouldn't feel that way. I strongly believe that I'm supposed to be home with my kids. I just needed that support. When I received *Volume Six* and started reading it, I read the whole thing right away! My kids were taking a nap and I just read. It's like it just fell into my lap because that's what I needed. It is exactly the encouragement I was looking for. After I read it, I was a more confident mom. And because I was a more confident mom, I think it rubbed off on my kids and my husband. And I think I am becoming a better mom. I can see more clearly the purpose in everything I do. Even though I'm not working outside the home, there are many contributions I can make to the Kingdom. For example, regular, everyday, tedious household tasks now have more meaning. I know I can obtain certain graces by doing the laundry or cleaning the floors. How awesome is that? My role actually IS important and this (*Volume Six*) validated it.

Please believe that if you are following the path to heaven, your children will also follow the path to heaven. A great deal of the work of parenting is done in the example that you set.
~Volume Six, June 10, 2004, Mary
(an unknown saint) Speaks to Mothers

Stacey G., IN

I feel so honored that I have this opportunity to discuss the *Volumes* with you. Thank you for writing this book of testimonies for *Direction of Our Times*. Also, thank Anne for me and tell her that I am grateful to her for sharing the Lord's messages with the world. It would take a lot of courage to do that. I am inspired by her faithfulness to the Lord, and I think she is such a beautiful person. I believe all the messages to be authentic. There is not anything written in the books that make me feel like I am being misled. The messages delivered in the *Volumes* are the same ideas, thoughts, feelings, and expressions that come to my mind when I think about Christ. Anne delivers the messages beautifully and they are written in a way that I think could only come straight from heaven. When I read the messages, the feeling I get can be described as euphoric. I often cry as I read because I feel the Lord with me and his love is just amazing. After reading *Volume One*, I took money out of my savings and bought 10 books to give family and friends. I wanted to share these wonderful messages with as many people as I could. I wrote a letter explaining the books and why I enjoyed them. Unfortunately, only a few people responded to the books. Most of them have not responded at all.

The *Volumes* have profoundly changed my life. Here is a list of some of the ways they have made a difference to me:

1. **Power of Prayer**- Before these books came into my life, I did not understand the importance of prayer. I did not pray very often because I did not want to bother God with the "little stuff." Now I understand that He wants us to come to Him with everything. It is now easier and more enjoyable for me to pray and I talk to God often throughout my day.

2. **Strengthened My Marriage**- My husband and I love to talk about the books together. We help each other on our spiritual journeys and try to encourage one another. We have read all the *Volumes*. I have read *Climbing the Mountain* (which is my favorite out of all the books) and *Mist of Mercy*. Ty is getting ready to read these soon. My husband is very busy but always makes time for his family and for the Lord. He is a teacher, coach, and is currently working on his Master's degree. Even though these things take up a lot of his time, Ty has made the *Volumes* one of his top priorities. He reads them during the

"read-in" sessions each day when the students are required to read for enjoyment and he also reads before he goes to bed at night. I was amazed when he told me that he makes time for these books at work.

3. **Strengthened My Faith as a Catholic**- Before reading the *Volumes*, I was not very active in my church. I would attend Mass most of the time, but did not take as much pride in the Catholic traditions as I do now. Anne taught me how to defend and appreciate my religion. While reading the books, I signed up to be a reader at church. I am generally a very shy person so I think that it surprised many people in the beginning (including myself!). I was always one of those kids that prayed the teacher would not call on me because I did not want to speak in front of the class! My priest told me right away that I am one of his best readers. The messages in the *Volumes* gave me the needed confidence and strength. The Lord has given me many graces by serving my church. Every time I go to the podium, I feel humbled to stand before the Lord's house and read His words. This has been one of the most gratifying experiences of my life.

My husband and I find it ironic that many times now when we finish discussing something we read in the books, our priest talks about it that weekend at mass! Sometimes the words and phrases he uses in his homily are right off the pages of the books. When this happens, I will kick my husband's feet to get his attention and he will then kick mine back. It seems like the Lord is using our priest to validate what we just read. We want to talk to our priest about the books but have not got to that point.

4. **Confession & Praying the Rosary**- In the fall of 2008, my husband and I went to confession for the first time in 12 years. The last time we went before that was for our Confirmations. Once again, I never understood how important this was until I read the Volumes. I know now that these are wonderful gifts from the Lord. Going to confession was an

uplifting experience for us. When I first went in, I was very nervous but my priest did a wonderful job so it ended up going well. I apologized for having not gone all those years. The priest's response was that was his fault, the church's fault, and not entirely my own. He said the Catholic Church is getting too relaxed about confession and needs to encourage people to go more often then they do. He then told me, "You must have received some very special graces to have come here today and this is something to be treasured." When my husband and I left our confessions, we were on cloud nine. We felt as if our souls were refreshed and we had a new start. It was an exciting time for us.

My husband is trying to say the rosary daily but I cannot say that I have gotten to that point yet. I really cannot explain why I do not make the time. I don't know why? It is something I need to work on. Rome was not built in one day so some things just take time. My husband told me something the other day that really inspired me. Ty has been praying the rosary lately during the read-in periods in class. He sits at his desk with his rosary and silently prays to himself. Some students have already asked him what he is doing. He says, "I am praying the rosary." As my sister likes to say, my husband carries a light. You would understand what I mean as soon as you met him. It does not matter to him what people think. He lives his life for Christ and is a great role model. People, especially kids, have always responded very well to Ty. His best service to the Lord is by the example he leaves for others.

5. **Closer Relationship with Christ**- Before reading the *Volumes*, I did not understand the depth of God's love for me. It brings me to tears to think about how much He loves me and knowing that He died on the cross for *me*.. I have talked to Jesus all of my life but always wondered how much He listened. I was intimidated and sometimes even fearful of Him. The books have taught me just how kind and forgiving He is.

Christ is our best friend and our biggest fan. No matter how many times we mess up, if we ask him, He is quick to forgive. The Lord's love for me takes my breath away.

6. **The Unimportance of Material Things**- When my father died, I watched the hearse drive past his farm and all the things he had worked for all his life. I took notice of the fact that there was no luggage rack on the Hurst. There is nothing in this life that we can take with us when we die. The only treasures we will have are the ones that we will find in heaven.

In *The Mist of Mercy,* Anne taught me the power of Satan and how he uses material things to pull us farther away from the Lord. Some things are obvious while other tactics are deceptive. In today's world of technical gadgets and the popularity of television and advertising, it is easy to go astray. After reading this book, I notice more than ever the evil that exists in all the things around me such as in music and TV. I understand the difference between "needs and wants" and am not finding pleasure in buying stuff like I used to. Don't get me wrong, I still like to shop from time to time but my outlook is different. I've never been a materialistic person, but I still have to pray to God often to help me to live simply and not look for happiness in things.

Through His grace, I am finding that my desire for things is being wiped away. This is a challenge sometimes for me and I have to go to Him about this often. Satan knows this and is working on me now more than ever. So it is important for me to keep going back to the Lord for help.

7. **Every Mother's Struggle**- When my first child was born, I struggled with the question;

Do I stay at home with him or should I work outside the home full time? *Volume Six* was one of my favorites. I felt like this book was written just for me. The Lord tells me to be home with my children (as long as it is financially possible) and how important it is to spend time with them. American culture does not support stay-at-home moms very well. I have received many rude comments from people and am always being asked, "What do you do all day?" After spending five years in college to earn three degrees, I can understand why people are so curious as to why I am not working outside the home.

This book has given me a lot of needed encouragement and has taught me that I am doing what is best for my family during this point in my life. I love page 11...

> *"Dear mothers, you must serve tirelessly. Those who have not experienced motherhood cannot understand how hard it can be to work, performing the same tasks over and over. When you perform these tasks in love, great graces can be obtained for both your family and for the Kingdom. In this way you are directly contributing to the advancement of the cause of heaven. Jesus is so pleased with this kind of cooperative service and He will reward you in countless ways. Cleaning your floors then becomes a divine service, as does washing your dishes, or cleaning the children's clothes, or any of the hundreds of domestic chores you perform daily."*
>
> ~Volume Six, page 11, Mary

When I get discouraged, I will "offer up" what it is I am doing. For example, when I am washing diapers, offering it up to the Lord makes the task go much easier for me! Because of this book and my prayers to the Lord, being a stay-at-home mom is no longer a battle I fight. I am proud of the sacrifices I have made to be with my kids and no longer care what the world thinks of me.

Note: Stacey has become my Facebook friend and it brings me so much joy to see this lovely young woman with her husband and children. God's love and peace shines in their faces and smiles.

Marie W., New Orleans, LA

I became aware of Anne by listening to her testimony when Archbishop Hannon interviewed her. I was very impressed. I hadn't read any of the books until someone gave me one. I was coordinating an event in New Jersey, came back to New Orleans (my home - this was after Katrina), and my house was a mess. I was running back and forth as much as I could to get it picked up.

The Lord planned I would be here for Mercy of God Sunday when Sister Briege McKenna was there. I went over to her and asked her to pray over me, which she did do. When she was finished praying, she asked me if I was familiar with the Anne books. I said yes, I was. She asked if I had read them, and I said no, but I have one. She said I needed to read it and I said OK. Two days later I left for New Jersey again. I knew where the book was and threw it in my suitcase and off I went. The pressure was tremendous with the job I had. I woke up in the middle of the night with terrible pain in my stomach. I knew it was nerves because of the pressure I was under. At that moment I remembered what Sister Briege told me and I went and picked up the Anne book, *Volume Two*. I read it and it was just like Jesus talking to me at that very moment. I read it three times and then fell into a deep sleep, an exhausted sleep, and was able to give everything over to the Lord that I was concerned about. It was a special message I felt that she had from the Lord for me because I didn't know I would be in that situation. This was in 2006 after Katrina hit. I had taken a job in New Jersey to coordinate a very large event at the Shrine of the Immaculate Heart of Mary, a Rosary Congress, with seven days and nights of prayer. But toward the end, everything began falling apart, although no one knew it but me. So I gave it all to the Lord that night and everything came out fabulous and the event was well attended. I was able to get from the Lord that this was an event I was planning, but not responsible for. The ability to let go and let God and recognize the fact that He was in control no matter how it turned out, it was up to Him.

(**Note**: In appendix information about Rosary Congress in New Orleans).

My children in this changing world, I want you to know that I am with you. I tell you this often, in many ways, because if you give consideration to the thought that your God is present in all that occurs, you will not feel frightened.
~Volume Four, January 14, 2004, God the Father

Susanne M., WI

God has given me many gifts throughout my life, including experiences as a nurse, a clown and storyteller. But when I started reading *Volume One*, reading about Anne's journey, I tried not to be envious. And then I realized Jesus was talking to *me*. I read the messages trying to savor them. I read them over and over again. I feel Jesus and the Blessed Mother so close. From that point on, everything in my life, including my prayer life has exploded. Fasting was never possible for me before. To receive the grace to fast is beyond words. I have received much grace in becoming a lay apostle. I get up every morning saying "yes." He has transformed my life. I've given up television. My heart would tell me this was something I didn't want to be watching. But then I gave up my movies. This was really hard because I have a movie collection of the old classics. A ripple went through my family because of this. It was very difficult for them even though they don't live with me. I'm also more careful about what I read. I don't read magazines. I try to stay away from the newspaper because I have sensed from Anne's messages Jesus wants us to be at peace. People have told me they see a lot of peace and joy in me. Of course, it's Jesus. I'm learning more and more to become aware of the presence of

God; how to reach out to Him; and speak with God as if He is my best friend. I had broken my leg a while back. That night in the emergency room, they sent me home on crutches and said I had to have surgery the next day. I couldn't take the pain pill. I had taken one around ten and it made me very sick. So, the entire night I had nothing for pain. And then I considered the Crucifix of Jesus. There He was and I remember reaching for Him. I am so glad for that night of pain. He has shown me in so many ways that suffering is not empty. I've learned that through Anne's messages. Jesus is teaching me about fear: I have nothing to be afraid of and to come to Him for everything.

I just turned 50 this year, and I made a pilgrimage to Medjugorje. When Our Blessed Mother throws a birthday party, there are no words to say how generous she was. I thought if I could just go to Medjugorje, maybe I wouldn't get to meet with the visionaries, but just be in their holy place and celebrate Mass with them. I wanted to listen to Father Jozo speak. I went with a group and we were able to meet with four of the visionaries, two of them when the Blessed Mother appeared to both at the same time. There were lots of tears. While climbing up Apparition Hill I heard there was part of the holy relic from Jesus' cross I really wanted to climb it. And, it did not look very easy to climb. I had broken my leg so I was on crutches at the time. One of the pilgrims who had been before told me she stopped at the 9th Station of the Cross and to not feel bad if I couldn't make it to the top. She said you are almost crawling after the 9th station it's so steep. Father Mark, a lovely priest, said he didn't know if I should try to climb the mountain. Well, I went right to Our Lord, right to the Adoration chapel. I asked Jesus what He thought. He told me to climb that mountain to the top and not be afraid because He would be with me every step of the way. And He was. And the Blessed Mother was. They got me to the top, cane and all. It took me four hours to the top and back down. It is so much like life as a lay apostle.

He says in all His messages He will not abandon us and He knows we are not perfect. I love it when He says He couldn't use us if we were perfect. If only more people understood the graces available to us now. The biggest thing I've learned from Anne is Jesus, our Blessed Mother and all of heaven are so close to us. All we have to do is look up and say yes.

If they accept their crosses in their lives, I can make them saints. Holiness is a process and suffering is part of that process. It is all about service to heaven, in suffering or in an absence of suffering.
~Climbing the Mountain, September 2, 2005, Jesus

Becky M.

I stopped going to church nearly the entire time I was in college. Then I met my husband after I graduated. We were married in my hometown six years later. The following year in that same church we buried my only brother who was killed in a motorcycle accident at the age of 26. This made my faith grow stronger but weakened my husband's. The following year we had a son. He was diagnosed with autism when he was four. This caused my husband to become extremely angry with God and he left the Church completely. I also stopped going to church because I didn't want to go alone. Two years later, I realized I needed to rely on my faith more and I entered a Familia group (a Catholic program committed to strengthening families) with a friend. This put me on the path of returning to church regularly. My son was about to enter the second grade, and my husband and I wanted him to make his first communion. I then started taking my son with me to church. One of the members of the Familia group brought the first Anne book to one of our meetings right around that time. She read from the book and it affected me. I bought the book a short while later. While reading *Volume One* about being on the bicycle, with God not letting us fall although we would wobble,

I completely lost it. The book spoke to me so directly I couldn't believe it. Although I had returned to church and had been in the Familia group, nothing put me on the spiritual path that I've been on like the Anne books have. I started reading them consistently and would pick one up opening to a random page, and it was as if God was speaking directly to me so completely. I just couldn't believe it. If my current difficulty would be about lack of patience, the reading would be about being patient and kind. If my current difficulty would be a temptation, the reading would be about remaining steadfast and resisting temptation. There were many times when my emotions would be strong clouding my judgment. I couldn't understand what I was feeling, and whatever I read in the Anne books would explain it to me. I can tell you that I strongly believe the presence of God has guided the writing and I hope my testimony helps to prove this.

If you are eating, I am there. If you are going to sleep at night, I am with you. You will never be in a place where I am not.
~Volume Six, June 21, 2004, Jesus

The next testimony is from a woman who, in an email, made me realize what a privilege it is to be handed the gift of writing this book by God Himself. After talking for hours to her while recording her testimony, she wrote, "You my dear have been a blessing to me, also and to many others who will read the testimonies of many. YOU were picked from heaven..Alleluia! Let us keep in touch...I do not mind being an adopted mother for you. It is very easy, all one has to do is to take on the heart of Mary, and listen and ponder and love...I think I can do that...Blessings from the Heart, Gloria." Gloria and I met in person for the first time about three months (and many conversations) after our initial contact at the Eucharistic

Day of Renewal in Justice, Illinois, June 2009. You couldn't miss her; a ray of sunshine came toward me and I jumped out of my seat straight into her loving arms. How is it that lay apostles love each other instantly? God's in charge here and knows just what He's doing...
~Bonnie

Gloria A., Syracuse, NY

In June 2006 I began immersing myself in the *Volumes*. This is how I got there:

I was preparing for the Sacred Heart Family Conference to be held in Syracuse, NY to celebrate the 100th anniversary of the Enthronement of the Sacred Heart of Jesus in the home. One day I went with my spiritual director, Monsignor John to Scranton, PA. He was the speaker on the Feast of the Sacred Heart vigil. He asked me if I would join him by sharing with the crowd information about the Sacred Heart conference; how important it was to the Lord, and why they should come, etc. So, I did. I gave the details and after finishing, I went back to the IHM (Immaculate Heart of Mary) convent where I was staying. I have a dear friend there, Sister Romaine who is in her 90's. She is quite a disciple of the Sacred Heart. She put me in my room and as I was preparing to retire, I turned on the tiny black and white television set. I found a Catholic program on called Focus. So I got my pajamas out and prepared to go to bed. A voice came on that I recognized and had admired for a long time, Archbishop Hannan. He was talking about a woman from Ireland with whom he really was impressed. He went on giving his testimony. Well, I sat there on the edge of my bed, holding my pajamas in my hand. I was so fascinated. I don't usually listen about other apostolate as I am so focused on and single-minded about the Sacred Heart and Enthronement. I opened myself up to what was being said because this really stirred me. And I thought, boy, I'd like to know more about that.

The next day I went home, celebrated the Feast of the Sacred Heart in the diocese and actually forgot about it (*DFOT*). I have no idea how or where, but I saw a little advertisement in a newspaper about a book called, *Thoughts on Spirituality*, Anne's first book. I really liked the title. I thought it sounded interesting. I'm always up for a good book about Jesus. So, I ordered the book. Can you imagine me sitting on my couch right near the image of the Sacred Heart, opened the package containing the book, opened the front cover and to my surprise, there was a letter from Archbishop Hannan. Well, I inhaled that book. I kept looking to see if Jesus were saying, 'to Gloria!' It was so personal. I laughed and cried. It was like new life was imparted to me through these words. I couldn't keep this to myself. So I called *DFOT* and ordered the gift packs. I sat down and thought to whom I wanted to send these. When I got them, I put a little notation to each person saying 'this is true. You can tell me yourself after reading them.' They changed my mind and my thinking. And many of those I sent have given their testimony. Once you open yourself up to Jesus speaking to you, you want to hear Him. But the greatest gift for myself (it's taken a little while) is a recorder in my mind. That's the only way I can describe it. For example, when I'm getting uptight or anxious, all of a sudden a passage from one of the messages I read two years ago comes to my mind. Talking about if you feel overburdened, (I'm paraphrasing), bring all your work to Me. Let me move you from one task to the next. And all of a sudden there is calmness. It has helped me to carry out my work. It's like a sign in front of me. Direction for the time we are in.

As I got more and more of the messages, I couldn't get enough. I found myself looking at the clock on the last day of the month, waiting for the monthly message to come. I've never looked forward to the first of the month in my life. One day I'm in my prayer chair, and I'm thinking, 'what else can I do (to help spread the messages)?' And then the answer came to me. I can bring them with me on every mission for the Sacred Heart. I go all over the country and beyond. I got up from my prayer chair and walked over to my computer and decided that I was going to email *DFOT* to tell them of this great idea. When I got to the website, and I don't know how this happened, but I'm sure heaven had a chuckle, somehow a message came up and said, "You may recognize my voice in these messages, but many do not hear my message. I want you to do everything you can to bring my messages forward." Something like that. I yelled out at the computer, 'Jesus, I was just going to tell you that!' And it was a confirmation that this is what He wanted me to do. To bring these *Volumes* out with me everywhere I go. That is exactly what happened. I have a special table set aside at missions and I keep an eye on it so if someone came to the table, I was there. People coming to the missions are very vulnerable. When they tell me their son is on drugs – that is an opportunity to give them the book on Addictions. When someone has lost a loved one – the book on Dying. It's all there. It has been an incredible opportunity of grace bringing the messages forward.

> *Each soul on earth has a path that has been traced out for him. His culture, his parents, his placement in time, all of these things have been designed by Me.*
> ~Climbing the Mountain, page 23, Jesus

Laura B., KS

I share this testimony as a reminder that God absolutely answers our prayers; and the time to pray is right now. The reason I had enough faith to come to this experience is *Climbing the Mountain* by Anne a lay apostle for Jesus Christ the Returning King. About 13 years ago my grandma, Anna (the person and saint my little girl Anna is named after) had some health issues that landed her in a nursing home. After just a year or two, there were a series of strokes that left her completely incapacitated (resembling the photos we saw of Terri Schiavo on TV--feeding tube, little-to-no brain activity, etc.). During those years I selfishly avoided visiting her and never prayed for her. I saw her about once a year on the average. My grandmother was a devout and loving Catholic woman.

Not long ago, at night, I began to read *Climbing the Mountain,* and during my prayers I kept thinking about Grandma. It was like God kept putting her in my thoughts, actually interrupting my other prayers. Again, I'm embarrassed to say I had never prayed for her before so it seemed strange that she kept coming to mind in such a random way.

After a few nights of this I began to feel like the Lord was "telling" me to go and pray with her. So, after church one day I told Doug (my husband) I just had to go see and pray with her. I decided I would pray the Chaplet of Divine Mercy. When I got there, I was so nervous. I had my oldest daughter Anna with me. This was unusual because with my baby being so little I generally always had him instead of one of the girls. (Funny that it happened to be "Anna" and not Molly). It was so long since I had been to the nursing home I was afraid they might have moved her and I wouldn't be able to find her. I wanted to avoid calling my mother to ask where grandma was because she would want to know why I was there after all this time, etc. Luckily, I found her room then started to change my mind about the whole thing. Nonetheless something in me, the Holy Spirit perhaps, strengthened me as I knelt beside her.

I took out my holy water bottle from MOMS (Moms Offering Moms Support) and blessed her hands and forehead with the sign of the cross. You need to know that I keep my rosary in a little leather pouch. Sad to say I have only had this rosary out of its pouch to show my girls and on my wedding day as I walked down the aisle with it in my hands. I turned the little pouch over to dump the rosary out in my hand and a medal fell out with it. IT WAS A MEDAL OF ST. ANN! I started to cry. I remembered someone had given me a medal a couple of years ago but honestly I hardly looked at it and just tossed it in the safest place I could think of--with my rosary. I had no idea that it was a St. Ann medal before that moment. I was shaking so much I could barely think.

I felt like God was saying, "You're doing exactly what I want you to. Go ahead." I then took out my little paper with "How to pray the Divine Mercy Chaplet" on it because I don't have it memorized and began to stumble along probably praying it all wrong. My little Anna stood beside me quietly the whole time holding the St. Ann medal. I finished the prayer after about 10 minutes, blessed Grandma again, kissed her forehead and said, "I love you" and we left. For the rest of the week God kept putting Grandma on my mind so I prayed nightly, "God please take her home to be with you. Please take her." She died one week later.

God works so fast. I don't know why I hadn't prayed for her a decade ago. I don't think it would have mattered. He had His purpose for her suffering and I can only honor that through my faith. I also told the Lord that I was concerned about telling this story but that I feel like I just want to tell it as a reason to renew faith in prayer. If I had not been reading *Climbing the Mountain* I'm not sure I would have been so connected to God's will in prayer. It's like Jesus is speaking right to you when you read the messages recorded and the story behind them. This is yet another reason why I love the Holy Catholic Church.

> ***Be at peace, My beloved apostles. The pain you suffer on earth, be it physical or emotional, will be utilized. I use each act of love, each little sacrifice.***
> ~Climbing the Mountain, page 37, Jesus

Rosemary N., NY

As I begin this writing, I have asked for inspiration from the Holy Spirit to please help me. How does one put into words what only the heart can speak? I will do my best. *Climbing the Mountain* was given to me as a Birthday gift from my Spiritual Director. This was the first I had heard of the mission of *Direction for Our Times* and Anne's profound experiences. Never did I realize the spiritual journey that would come about from the placement of that book into my hands.

We know how mysteriously and wonderfully God works. It "just so happens" that unknown to any of us -two of my closest friends were reading *Climbing the Mountain* at the same time I was. Needless to say, we knew that Jesus was at work here, and it wasn't long before we formed our monthly group and have been meeting faithfully one Sunday a month for about two years. Our little group has five members total, and that includes Marisa, the young daughter of one of our members who is just 7 years old. (She joined us when she was 5!)

The greatest impact this mission has had on my life would most definitely be on the personal relationship that I have with Jesus. I have always strived to live a good and holy life as best as I could. I had come to realize that Jesus is really someone who wants me to know Him on a personal basis, and I wanted this as well. While I tried to work on this relationship, I was often plagued with "scruples" and feelings that I had to be perfect, which stood in the way of any meaningful spiritual progress. Then I met Anne. Her relationship with Jesus was so refreshing. She was so honest and good, and yet so human. She was not a "living Saint" but someone, like myself, who was doing her best. I loved the relationship she had with Jesus, and how His great love and compassion, His desire to guide and encourage her, was so apparent. When I began to read Jesus' words to her, I no longer felt that I was reading a book. Now Jesus was speaking directly to my heart, to me personally.

Everything made sense. I found answers to what troubled me – I found my purpose. Jesus made me realize that I was part of a greater plan; that I counted. How consoled and encouraged I was to read that I had all of heaven helping me to do my part, and that I didn't have to be perfect to bring about the change Jesus wanted in this world.

When I am troubled and disturbed, it never fails that I come to a message in whatever *Volume* I happen to be reading. Jesus addresses the "exact" concern I am having at that moment and consoles me. I am once again filled with hope and am reminded to "walk by faith, not by sight." I am made aware through the readings that Jesus is in control and that change is coming about. It is incredible and always leaves me in awe of His great power and love. How can one read these *Volumes* where Jesus speaks to the individual's heart, and continue to be afraid?

When I had begun this mission, spending even ten minutes before the Tabernacle was hard for me. Now I look forward to my weekly Holy Hour and it is the most precious time of my week. I have learned to "just be" with Jesus. It is so different from the days of mechanical prayers and trying to fill up the time with pious actions. Now I come to Jesus as a little child who just wants to be with Him. How He welcomes us as a child! The joy of humility has also been brought home to me through these *Volumes*. I am learning more and more of the dangers of pride, of holding onto my own ideas which keeps one "closed" and "unteachable." If anything, the readings only open up to me how very much I do not know, and how very much there is for me to learn and experience. My prayer now is to remain open and teachable. From the beginning of this journey, I was so consoled by Jesus' words telling me not to be concerned about my family. He lovingly tells me that I am to do my work for Him and He will take care of them. He goes further to say that the desires of my heart become the desires of His heart. I cannot begin to express in words the miracles that

He has brought about. The longing of my heart has been to have a good relationship with my son and his wife, and all my efforts to bring this about were fruitless, or actually made matters worse! But then, I read and believed Jesus' words to me. I follow His directions as best as I can and put my heart into working for Him, while leaving my loved ones in His hands. I sit in awe at what He has done. A relationship more loving than I dreamed possible is unfolding between my son and daughter-in-law.

My staying in the background and leaving all to Jesus has brought them forward. My little grandchildren are a gift in all of this, and they love and know their "Nanny." They sense my great love for them. I believe the new love that Jesus has instilled into my heart through this mission is what my family is responding to. But perhaps the greatest joy of finding Jesus through these writings is the experience of His great mercy. Mercy not only for me, but for everyone. He wants   me to have mercy as well – to bring Him those souls who suffer from confusion, rejection, and painful experiences. How much Jesus thirsts for souls, and this I am learning is the mission He has for me – to bring Him as many souls   as possible. Again, in humility, I am powerless to do this, but with all of Heaven working with me, Jesus makes all things possible.

All in all, it is such a joy to know that Jesus is doing so much in me! He is using me, as imperfect as I am, He has chosen me to help Him in this mission. He is giving me all I need to accomplish His work, and I stand in awe as hearts are touched and lives are changed.

Apostles are not called to be judges but delivery people. If we deliver Jesus to souls He Himself will correct them, tutor them, and illuminate their path on the mountain."

~Climbing the Mountain, pg. 64, Anne, a lay apostle

Patricia P.

I believed I was a good Catholic because I never missed Mass, went to confession once a year, and prayed the rosary. After reading, *Climbing the Mountain*, I began attending daily Mass, praying the rosary the Divine Mercy Chaplet, and the Liturgy of the Hours. I am a member of my parish "Cenacle" group that meets once a week for an hour of prayer. I also receive the Sacrament of Reconciliation once a month. The ladies of my church are currently conducting a study of the aforementioned book, and we are greatly anticipating discussing the impact it has had and still has on our lives. I read it in two days. I did feel that Jesus was speaking directly to me. It made me cry, gave me great comfort, and made me eager to be a lay apostle of "Jesus Christ the Returning King."

Like all families in this day and age, the majority of my family and friends do not practice their faith. The greatest consolation I derived from Jesus, while reading this book, was that I, by my prayers, could bring about the salvation of my loved ones. I also look forward to the monthly message. It always seems to say exactly what I need to hear at that time. Lastly, my niece who had been away from the church for over 25 years, returned to the Sacraments, after the death of her grandmother. She is now reading *Climbing the Mountain,* and attending the study group. She and I will continue our spiritual journey together and pray that others in our family, through graces from Jesus, will return to the fold.

> *"Be hopeful and patient when you pray for the conversion of a soul. Remember that when he returns, he can make the greatest strides in holiness in a short period of time. This is yet another reason to be filled with joy."*
> ~Climbing the Mountain, page 67, Anne, a lay apostle

M. M., UK

When my friend gave me *Climbing the Mountain*, she said it was written by a "visionary from Ireland." I think because I am Irish she thought I would be interested. When she handed it to me, my first thought was Ireland needs another visionary like a hole in the head! ("sorry Anne!") I was wondering how to get it back to her as soon as possible as I wasn't interested in any more superstitious things. I decided she was a good friend and I don't like to lie. I would read the first paragraph/page and give it back to her, saying thanks, but no thanks.

At the first paragraph, I felt this was genuine, but continued reading it looking for "holes" or anything contrary to what I knew the Church was teaching or didn't feel right. I never found anything; it was wonderful, and answered questions I never had answered before. It completed the little understanding I had, so everything fit into place better. I loved it. Also when I was reading the book, Anne described souls at the tomb contemplating the power of God "as if for millions of years." That night when I read St. Faustina's diary and she said exactly the same thing. I thought that this coincidence was too significant to ignore.

I had been going to an Adoration chapel for 30 minutes a week, which I loved. Then one day the thought occurred to me that I would get more out of it, if that's the right way to put it, if I went for an hour. That night when I was reading CTM, the page I was on said lay apostles should spend 1 hour per week in Adoration. I was stunned at the speed in which God confirmed my little thought.

When I started to read the *Volumes*, I felt that they were so uplifting; directing without condemning. They were from God and when I read *Volume Four,* I felt I could almost hear the Father speaking. The strength in His voice was tangible.

I found the books down to earth and described how I was feeling, my struggles and failings. Also when I had a problem I would look at Jesus and say, "I need help" and open one of the *Volumes*, and invariably it would be so specific to what I needed. On one occasion I had five problems in an ascending order of priority. I opened one of the *Volumes*, and incredibly Jesus answered each problem through the page, and in the order I had put them in!!

In a world of discouragement and panic, the words in the *Volumes* encourage and give me a way to proceed, they help me see that I am trying, and that when I fail, I am still loved, I feel that they instill a confidence and calm that Jesus is working, and He will give me what I need, when I need it.

> *"My dear friend, notice that Jesus calls you His apostle. He is asking you to serve Him. Do not make the mistake of thinking that He is talking to someone else. He is talking to you. There is work for you in the kingdom."*
> ~August 1, 2005, St. Barnabas Climbing the Mountain,

Janet B., MI

From the moment I heard about Directions for Our Times from a friend and the promises of Jesus to pursue complete conversion of each of our loved ones, I knew I was going to be a lay apostle. I began reading *Climbing the Mountain, Mist of Mercy* and the *Volumes*. The words I'd heard many times in my life actually came alive for me now. I felt Jesus and the apostles speaking directly to me. My thoughts of Jesus are different now.One of my sons was going to church for reasons other than to know God. His life was very difficult in the past year and he is still struggling, but through the *Volumes* he was introduced to *Direction for Our Times*. He is learning so much. I know that Jesus keeps his promises when I look at my son.

Jen S., WI

I found myself in the Adoration Chapel and was saying to our Lord, "You know, Lord, I seem to be doing so much talking all the time. I sure wish I could hear more from You." Within a short period of time, I found myself going to Holy Hill Shrine in Wisconsin. Sister Briege McKenna was there with *Volumes* at the back of the church. I remember taking the (*DFOT*) newsletter as *Volume One*, the one I wanted, was all sold out. I work in a gift shop and after reading the newsletter, I ordered the *Volumes*. I cannot tell you how many *Volumes* I have given out to other people and hearing how they feel as if the Lord is speaking to them. One of those people was my sister-in-law. We sent her three of the *Volumes* for Christmas. When her husband died, she said if it hadn't been for the *Volumes* she wouldn't have gotten through it all. She kept reading through them with her husband and weeks before he died he wanted to go to confession. After that he was in hospice for less than a week and was gone. She says the *Volumes* have been so important in her life. *Volume Two,* has deepened my relationship with Jesus. It has made the Eucharist and Our Lord's presence more alive. By saying the Allegiance Prayer every day I am more conscious of God and what He wants me to do. I know our Lord is calling us to be open. And, by being open we need to listen. I find Him confirming what He asks of me. I know it's from Him and not my ego.

> *I want My children to be calm. Even in My service, My children tend to rush to and fro, as though this life were a race. My children, when you are hurrying, I cannot help you to listen.*
> ~Volume Two, September 1, 2003, Jesus

Barb, IN

I moved to St. John, Indiana, when my youngest was only a baby. My faithlife was pretty bad and I was having a hard time with it. I kept going into the Adoration chapel and asking God to give me something, some kind of a sign. Then one day, I received *Volume One* in the mail. It came from an older woman who I really did not know. I didn't think anything of it and put it aside for about six months. One week before chapel I decided that I needed something different and picked up the book. I started to read it in chapel, I couldn't put it down. It's like it was talking directly to me. I kept asking God, "Is this really real? Are you really speaking through this person, Anne? Are you really speaking to me?"

Then one Sunday in mass I couldn't seem to focus on what Father was saying during his homily. I kept thinking about the book. Then when I would try to focus, it seemed as if he were directly quoting from the book. All of a sudden it was as if I heard in my being something like "I have always had prophets, why would I leave you now." It was as if the Holy Spirit just came down and gave me what I needed for my faith. I have more faith now than I have ever had. And I think it all started with the prayer to God asking for a sign and receiving the book.

Many souls are crying out for Me. They think I do not hear. It is they who do not hear. They are not listening for My voice, which must be heard in the silence of their heart.
~Volume One, page 83, Jesus

Annette T., LA

I am married to a wonderful man with three great boys. My story starts in 2004-2005. I was a registered pharmacist and having trouble with my hands. I started having pain that would prevent me from typing. It gradually worsened and the pain radiated up to my lower and upper arms, up my shoulders to my neck. The pain increased so much by the Fall of 2005 that I could no longer type at all. I could not hold a telephone to my ear, drive a car, fold clothes, and take care of most of the necessities to run a family. I would show up at work and pretty much stand there. I could only work two to three hours a day before the pain became too great, then I had to get home and lie down. I saw many doctors, and each one would tell me how healthy I was, but could tell me nothing about where my pain originated. After the 12th doctor giving me the same speech, I broke down crying in the doctor's office. How could this be? I was a vibrant young working mother with a great career; what was happening? At this time, my mother-in-law gave me *Volume One,* by Anne, a lay apostle. I couldn't put it down. Here was another soul struggling as I was. She also had health problems and pain that mystified doctors. I was so touched by her path and her faith. Once I started to read the messages given by Jesus, it touched me deep within my soul. My God was speaking to me. I knew beyond a shadow of a doubt, that He was calling me, calling me closer to Him. Within a short time, I finished *Volume One,* and immediately found a book store and bought the rest of the *Volumes* and *Climbing the Mountain.*

I have never read spiritual books that reach the simplicity and beauty as these books. In each message, Jesus spoke to me where I was. From these *Volumes,* He answered the many questions pouring out of me. Most important was the peace. Within the time that I read these books, Jesus slowly took the chaos of my illness, and replaced it with His peace. I stopped searching for answers in the world, and turned to Jesus. Within several months, my family doctor was able to find a medication that stabilized the pain and now enables me to live my life as before, except for one thing. My life had changed. I am not who I was. This pain had taken me on a wonderful spiritual journey that I could never have imagined. In my heart, I knew I had to share what had happened to me.

I am with you, child. I feel your weakness and sickness and will adjust your responsibilities accordingly. This will pass. Offer your suffering to Me so that I can nourish souls, especially souls who are in error and in danger of falling away. My heart aches for them.

~Volume One, page 87, Jesus

Kathy F.

Sometimes I love to read the messages as a love letter, hearing how much God does love us and yearns for us. He makes it simple.

I, Jesus, love every person ever created by the Father. I seek goodness and peace for every man and woman on earth.
~Jesus, Monthly Message, November 1, 2008

Prior to *DFOT* sending out the request for testimonies, I inquired about interviewing lay apostles in Hawai, as I was tagging along with my husband on a business trip. I was given several names and emails, and Pam responded quite quickly. We arranged to meet at her church, St. John Vianney in Kailua, for 9:00am Mass. She and her husband Michael graciously welcomed us into their home for the interview. I could have stayed and talked to Pam all day. Her openness and honesty was refreshing. I only wish we didn't live so far apart...~Bonnie

Pam A., Kailua, HI

My friend, Susan, whom I sponsored in RCIA, asked me to explain a book for her about this lady Anne. She sent me *Climbing The Mountain*, and I knew after reading it, this was real. Soon after my husband told me that with the way the economy and tourism was, he was worried why his boss asked him to lunch. I was in prayer and I said, Lord, what does this mean? What are we going to do? Then I thought about CTM and how all of heaven was on our side and ready to help. So, I decided that if I could find my sunglasses, I'd believe anything! I was requesting this from all of heaven. I had been looking for three weeks, everywhere, including the grocery store, the bank and the video store. I got up from my prayer chair and walked right to them! I said, "Oh my, thank you Lord. You are planning something new here." So, I finished CTM and then Susan sent me a couple of the CDs. I began to listen to them in my car. I would go online to listen to them. She later sent me a couple of Volumes. I read those. Then someone bought me an iPod. So, now I have Jesus on my iPod. I just listen over and over. I don't want to miss a thing. I gave a copy of the CD's to my pastor. I also gave him a printout of the Volume for priests. The Lord has confirmed over and over in these books, showing me myself. It's very easy, after 32 years in the Lord, to think you have it made in the shade, thinking I must be close to sainthood! But then the Lord revealed the fear in me. And the Humility prayer...I love it! The first time I read it, I thought, I can't pray this! But it's the desire of and the fear of. Desire keeps you from being who the Lord calls you to be. Fear keeps you from saying what you need to say.

I now look back over my prayer journals and see I wrote a lot of what Jesus is saying now, but it's more than just words. It's something I know. I get the fact that Jesus is always with me. I get going to Him for everything. I get asking Him to give me His joy when I have none and asking the angels and saints for help. I've experienced the closeness of heaven. He's confirmed His words over and over to me. People see me differently, too. I'm hearing all sorts of things, and I know it's the presence of the Lord in me.

"There is only one path for us, after all, and if our destination is Jesus, we will only feel confident and at peace on the most direct track to Him."
~Climbing the Mountain, page 75, Anne

I returned home from running errands one day and my husband said I had missed a call from a Scottish woman having trouble emailing her testimony to me. I dialed the number to return her call. The minute we spoke, I knew God placed Maureen and her husband Richard in my life for a reason. After many wonderful telephone conversations with Maureen, I discovered they come to Fort Myers (where I reside) every year to watch the Red Sox in training camp. We made plans to have Richard and her for dinner with two other lay apostle couples. Our personal meeting was just as it had been on the telephone. The week after our visit Maureen called me early one morning. She said Jesus put a message in her heart for me and to get pen and paper to write it down. This was the message: "My beloved bonny lassie, I have called you to follow Me as a fisher of souls. I send you forth to catch many who are lost, many who are floundering, many who are now falling into the depths of the darkness of despair in these serious times. Be My Light. Be My Hope. Be My Joy. I am Victor. I am Lord, the loving fisherman." The impact this message had on me right in the middle of collecting testimonies was tremendous. ~Bonnie

Maureen M., MA

Being open to God's grace, I have been blessed being called into this Lay Apostolate in God's Kingdom, at this time in my life. Receiving the picture of God's Mountain on the Litany of Humility card took me back twenty years. During those years I have discovered that often Our Good God reveals His plan of what He wills to do in the future!

Over twenty years ago I was with our parish prayer group at a retreat house on a lake in Massachusetts. After Mass our spiritual director Father Laughlin suggested that we go outside as it was such a beautiful morning, and sit in the Presence of the Lord. He was right! It was beautiful! As I sat on a large rock at the edge of the lake, a great peace came over me, and as I looked at the bright blue sky, felt the warmth of the sun, I closed my eyes and began to praise God for the beauty of His creation. Then something happened as never before. I felt myself as a child holding the hand of my Creator. We were at the top of the mountain! He invited me to look down the mountain through His Glorious Light. This light flowed over the top of the mountain to the ground so beautifully. Then, to my horror, the light was becoming dissipated by a creeping darkness, coming from the ground toward His Holy Mountain.

Immediately, I was filled with deep sobs of sadness. I asked the Lord what had happened and He said, "It is the darkness of sin that is gradually covering the earth." I closed my eyes as I did not want to see what was happening. When I closed my eyes, I heard a quiet voice say, "Look now." As the Lord spoke, suddenly it seemed as if stars were falling from His Hand which sparkled on the dark ground. Then, they seemed to grow into little pools of light, and in them groups of people with a central figure leading them. First of all, I saw Pope John Paul II, then local priests, religious and laity. All were sharing the gift of light they had received. Gradually, the pools of light overflowed into each other making a broad "stream of light," and all began to march up the mountain singing joyfully with their arms raised. Just beyond the stream was a grey area, and beyond that great darkness. I was led to understand those in the grey area wanted to be in the light, but did not know how to get there by themselves. I had a strong feeling they were family members and friends. Then I saw people nearest to the grey area begin to lift up those with their arms up asking for help. All were passed in to the middle of the stream and carried up with love. The stream widened, and those in the darkness slipped away. Where there was sadness and uncertainty, there was fullness of joy for all the mountain climbers! I sat for a long time praying in thanksgiving for what had happened.

When I met with Father Laughlin he asked me if I wanted to share my time of meditation with him. I replied that I had experienced a wonderful vision and was feeling overwhelmed. As he listened, I closed my eyes to replay the beauty of the vision, believing it was genuine, but wondering if I had projected myself into it. Opening my eyes, he looked at me and said, "What you envisioned is Biblical. Go and ponder *Isaiah 2:2-5.*"

"In days to come, the mountain of the Lord's house shall be established as the highest mountain and raised above hills. All nations shall stream towards it; Many people shall come and say: Come, let us climb the Lord's mountain, to the house of the God of Jacob, that he may instruct us in his ways, and we may walk in his paths."

As I read, my heart started pounding. I had lived the experience of God's people "streaming" toward the mountain, ascending it together, and bringing others with them. Little did I know then, that at this time, with countless others, I would become a lay apostle living the message to bring others into His Kingdom. May the Lord be praised!

> *"We climb the mountain through our daily 'yes' to Jesus."*
> ~Climbing the Mountain, pg. 5, Anne

Catherine B., MI

Jesus has a great sense of humor. And I think He likes my sense of humor, too. That's why we are getting along so well! He put me in my job for a reason, so I could reach out and help people. I couldn't understand how I went from my past occupation, which was working with high-end people in casinos to this job in social services. I trust the Lord by living in each moment. I realize He has the grace, no matter what the situation, to get me through every moment.

When I'm dealing with my clients, I'll walk out and ask the Lord how he wants me to help this person. From there, I know what to do. We (Jesus and I) have a "working" relationship.

> *"We must spend time in silence and ask Jesus and He will tell us where our path lies on this mountain*

of holiness. Most of us need to look no further than to our vocations and it is always best to begin at that point."

~Climbing the Mountain, page 5, Anne

Christina A., Sweden

I am not much of an apostle, but I do feel as though Jesus is speaking directly to me through the messages. It is great, wonderful and encouraging. Jesus comes nearer to me. He becomes more alive, only I have to respond more truly.

Debbie C.

I thank my mother every day that I am blessed with her and the faith she has bestowed upon me. She introduced two books and the *Volumes* over a year ago, and they have brought me closer to Jesus with a new and clearer understanding of His wishes. I now worry less and have witnessed conversions and miracles within my own family. I cannot express enough how grateful I am for my daily growth and the words from Jesus and all of Heaven. The ability to feel Jesus is talking to me - I am completely and utterly honored and have an increased realization of the mercy of God and all the support that Heaven provides.

Barbara S.

After I read the first book of Anne's series, *Thoughts on Spirituality*, I had a firm desire to join *Direction for Our Times*, simply because of Jesus' promise that my children would return to the Church if I would become His apostle. I had been praying for this exact thing for quite a long time. I did feel like Jesus was speaking directly to me as He said, "Just sit back and watch me work."

My life changed as I began to religiously take part in the five steps that lay apostles of Jesus Christ, the Returning King, agree to perform.

Within a relatively short time, my granddaughter informed me that my daughter-in-law, the wife of my youngest son, was reading the Anne books. Within the year, my daughter-in-law converted from the Lutheran Church and brought her husband back into the Church as well as their two small children. Today, they are active members of Immaculate Conception Catholic Church; truly a modern day miracle for which I give grateful praise and thanksgiving to my Jesus.

The next testimony is near and dear to my heart. It is from my younger sister who had drifted away from her Catholic roots and was floundering about looking for answers. And, she found them within the *Volumes*. Her transformation and her daughters' happened right before my eyes. My nieces latched on to the words of Christ as if finding a new friend. I was given the honor of being Hayley and Maddy's sponsor as they received their first Holy Communion and Confirmation. As we were processing down the aisle with the other candidates, Maddy whispered to me with tears in her eyes, "Aunt Bonnie, I am finally going to receive Jesus!" I just hugged her tight, fighting back tears of joy...I am so proud of them all and their commitment as lay apostles.

Sheryl K., CO

I had a rough night, it seemed like I was being pulled in too many directions: unholy paths, impatience, and fighting with my inner self. I have always believed in God and prayed every day, or so I thought. While I had stopped going to church, I knew that my kids needed God in their lives, but I was feeling helpless, hopeless, depressed and overwhelmed.

I have always looked up to my sisters. They have raised me, regularly giving me advice, even when I didn't want it. They are always there to talk to me and help me, but I was crying out for help. I needed God back in my life. Over the years, I noticed changes in all my sisters, each having a deep commitment to God. This is where it began for me. I was talking on the phone to my sister, complaining about my children, work, life..."Why me?" I used to say. That very day my sister shared the loving words of Jesus Christ from a series of books called the *Volumes*, also known as – Anne's books. My sister said, "Sheryl, what's missing in your life is a relationship with God. Get online now, this very second, and make a commitment to me. Read at least one page a day. Promise me, she repeated over and over." She was going to mail *Volume One* to me right away. As much as I was resistant and thinking I didn't have the time, I went online and read the first page. I was stunned and printed 50 pages. Then, I sat rekindling my relationship with God.

The impact of *Volume One* was astounding. I began to see and deal with my issues, my two little girls, my family, and coworkers in a new light. This book made sense of things. Clearly, this is what I was missing.

I began to read a page a night to my girls. They have grown so close to God because now they have Him every day in their lives. Hayley, my 13 year old, now says when being bullied or hurt, "Mom, they are God's children, and I must love them." It truly amazes me.

Even though the messages from Our Lord were impactful, I found myself slipping back into old habits. One night I was playing an addictive game on the computer when my youngest daughter, Maddy, 10 years old, was trying hard to get my attention. Engrossed in the game, I ignored her plea. She needed me to talk with her, comfort her, and pay attention to her. I was being selfish and told her to go to bed and after my game I would come to tuck her in. When I finished and went to her, she was crying. I hurt her feelings. She felt like I loved the computer more than her. I told her that was ridiculous, but needless to say I felt small and horrible. Lying in bed that night, I reached for Anne's book and randomly opened it; sure as anything it talked about how kids are number one. Spend time with your kids; kids must be first. It even said turn off the computer and love your kids. Give them the gift of your time because they need you now. Wow! So many times I think this book was written for me. It also makes me realize I am not perfect, nor does God expect me to be. I am just practicing, and I love that line.

Now months later, I feel like a much stronger person. I give up my days to God and let Him lead me where He wants. I am proud, no, I am blessed to say these books have changed my life and my girls too. We are followers of Jesus Christ. Thank you, my sissy, and thank you God for bringing Anne's work to all of us.

Cecilia A., Philippines

I love the messages of Jesus, the monthly messages, and those that come from the *Volumes* and other books of Anne. Yes, I feel like Jesus is directly talking to me. And whenever I am faced with some worries or anxiety, I remember His messages, especially when He says, "do not be afraid" and "don't worry about the future". I always console myself with His words "Trust Me." I remember His admonition: "whenever you do something, ask me first," although at times I fail to practice this. But I know He takes me for what I am, and He sees me still striving to be better. Surprisingly, I find myself saying the same admonitions to others!

Lilibeth C., Philippines

I sincerely feel that Jesus directly speaks to me and it touches my being. My husband, for 4 years now, has been into dialysis treatment twice weekly and regularly. I testify that GOD truly provides! Both of us are jobless but, through our generous close relatives (especially our three adult children, my sister and mother), plus some government institutions, a spiritual mother and others who occasionally give - to date we never skip his treatments. By the way, last night I was given money ($1,000.00) for my husband's medications and I placed it, first at the left tiny pocket of my red jeans and transferred it to the right fearing the hole on the left pocket. When I reached the house, I searched for it and found it missing. My fear happened. It disturbed me but due to the messages, I was consoled in thinking that God gives and God takes away. Because of pride in myself and not being grateful to God, I must admit I was far from thinking about HIS goodness and I believe it happened so I could reflect more on His presence at all times.

> *But if, through no fault of your own you suffer poverty, I assure you today that if you accept this in peace I will reward you beyond your furthest imaginings. In places where people are poor, I am there with My greatest graces. Dear beloved ones, believe Me today when I tell you that people who come to heaven do not regret anything they suffered on earth. Rest in this thought.*
> ~Heaven Speaks to Those Who Suffer From Financial Need, December 17, 2006, Jesus

Jo Ann O., FL

One evening, we had friends over to watch Anne's DVD, titled, *Climbing the Mountain*. After our friends left, I was discussing the DVD with my husband and I was wondering why we do not see greater evidence of the Saints interceding for us in our lives. I decided to try an "experiment" on myself. I would give the Saints plenty of time to work on me! My idea was to spend 1 hour daily in front of the Blessed Sacrament. My schedule changed, and on the days that I worked, I would get up at 5:00 am and spend an hour in prayer at home. Well, the Saints didn't waste any time. The first morning, I was able to spend an hour in the Chapel, go to daily Mass and still get to work on time. Within three hours at work, I was humiliated on two different occasions. I almost laughed out loud when I realized they were showing me immediately that humility was definitely needed for my spiritual walk to progress.

Over the next two weeks, Jesus gently and lovingly showed me areas of my life in which some decisions I had made, hurt other people. If I had spent time "listening" to Him on a regular basis, I definitely would have made better choices.

It has been six months since I began my "experiment" and I cannot even begin to tell you all the beautiful things I have learned. The secret is so simple, give God the time and He will work miracles in our lives. I have always felt that I never had enough time to get everything done in my day. He has helped me to understand, that <u>nothing</u> else is more important than spending time with Him.

I have been "Martha" (busy in the kitchen) all my life and now with His grace, I have become Mary (sitting at His feet). And yes, the Saints definitely do work in our lives if we just give them the "time".

"We must never underestimate what Jesus can do for us and we should understand that Jesus will take us in any condition."
~Climbing the Mountain, page 112, Anne

RoseAnn O., PA

I find the messages to be most touching and tender and always pertinent to my life. It really is as though Jesus is speaking to my heart personally. I always start the day with the Allegiance prayer, morning offering, prayer for the Holy Father and prayer to the holy angels. Those beautiful prayers seem to bless my day. The prayers and messages are comforting and consoling in a world too busy to hear the voice of Jesus.

Rose P.

The monthly messages have truly helped me feel closer to Jesus. The messages seem to be directly related to a need or to personal doubts and troubles. It's as though our Lord sent the messages just for my healing. They have helped me to love Jesus more deeply and sustained me through many dark times.

Norma G.

It's unbelievable. In every message I read, I not only feel as though Jesus is speaking directly to me, but I can almost hear His voice. And everything He says is so pertinent. I also feel as though I am living my Catholic faith with much more conviction and am very proud to be Catholic.

> *Dearest apostles, if you give me your full commitment, there is no limit to what I can do.*
> ~Jesus, Monthly Message, October 1, 2009

Maria F., Faroe Islands

I first heard about *Direction For Our Times* through Sr. Briege McKenna when she visited the Faroe Islands in July 2007. I have read several of the books regarding the messages. Their depth and simplicity have inspired and nourished my faith. I say the Daily Offering Prayer each morning and have found that it helps me to be more aware of Jesus working through me and of his love for me.

I also subscribed to the monthly message in 2007, and I have been deeply touched, even amazed, sometimes by the accuracy of the messages with regard to my state of mind and being. I felt that Jesus was speaking directly to me through a specific word, phrase or reference to something deeply personal within me. At such times, I felt Jesus' love and compassion.

Lorna J.

I read the monthly messages and whatever the message is saying seems to fit into my life at the present moment. Sometimes I won't pick up the message straight away, printing it out to read later. But you can guarantee that at the time I eventually read the message, it will be relevant to me at that moment in time. I read more religious books, etc. now and it's as if I am being led. The jigsaw all fits together as by an unknown hand which I believe to be the Holy Spirit.

Yolanda H., TX

Ever since I have been getting the monthly messages, I feel they are in response to a need or a prayer I have. His notes of encouragement are exact and meaningful and help me focus on my spiritual life just where I need it. Other times I note that He must have been hiding in my home and seeing my many stumbles and falls and subsequently He delivers His next message. His guidance and understanding help me to see my failings with a heavenly perspective, and I can quickly pick myself up whereas before I had such a hard time forgiving myself.

The messages are helping me develop a healthier self-image of who I am in God's eyes. Like a good Father, He lets us know exactly why we suffer and that suffering is part of the plan. Sometimes I say, "Lord, you must need this suffering for someone or something today and since I can barely pray, I offer it to you as my prayer and with my love." On my good days, I feel that others are stepping up to take the suffering I am not having that day and feel grateful to those who are undergoing the suffering.

> *What comes from Me can only be good. When you see goodness and kindness, you must thank Me. When you see mercy and compassion, you must thank Me. These occurrences originate in heaven and are brought to earth through the participation of those who cooperate with grace."*
> ~Jesus, Monthly Message, June 1, 2009,

Karin C., UK

Reading of your request for testimonies really challenged me. Where would I start? I had never thought to itemize all the things that spoke so deeply into my being – new things that Jesus revealed through Anne's writings and the monthly messages. Since I found my own personal relationship with Jesus in the Renewal during the early 70's, Jesus often "spoke His Word" into my prayers, which I believe was the reason why I immediately felt comfortable with Anne's writings. Heaven became more real than I could ever have imagined. The vision of all Heaven's involvement together with the firm promise of help in difficult times is of great comfort and allays many a secret fear. I am continually experiencing new revelations of God's amazing love for me, for all His people, for all the world – a new awakening accompanied by an undeniable assurance of God the Father, Jesus and the Holy Spirit in full control.

As a non-Catholic with twenty years teaching experience in a Roman Catholic school and many dear Catholic friends, the fragmentation of the Church has long been a burden on my heart. Seeing the apostolate of Jesus Christ the Returning King increase so fast and hearing Jesus' words of encouragement have given me a heightened expectation to see an accelerated growth towards Christian unity.

Last but not least, and indeed the cause of my great new-found joy, is the humbling realization that I can be of use in the saving mission of Jesus, and that God has a multitude of unseen ways to involve my actions and attitudes in ways I could never have dreamed of. I believe that every aspect of my faith has been affected in a most positive way.

In the very first DFOT newsletter, Fall 2005, there is a Q & A section for Anne. After reading the previous testimony from a non-Catholic, I felt it necessary to supply Anne's reply to this question:

Q: I'm not Catholic. Can I be part of this work?

ANNE: Yes, of course. Our Lord is calling all to become His apostles. If your Christian community does not have Confession, then that obligation is not applicable to you. You do not have to be a Catholic to say the rosary, or to offer your day to Jesus. If Jesus Christ is calling out to you, you will know. To me, a Christian is a Christian is a Christian. Period. We all just have different ways of worshiping and praising Jesus Christ. There should be no walls between us.

You have come to trust My loving compassion, My forgiveness and My uninterrupted affection. That is because you have come to know Me.
~ Jesus, Monthly Message, March 1, 2009

Laurianne S., Aberdeen, Scotland

I must say I have never left the Church, had any illness physically or felt 'away' from God to claim that the messages have healed me in that respect. But what I can say, is that they have definitely been talking directly to me. I had never heard of Anne until my sister Michelle started forwarding the monthly messages and sharing them with me. When I read them it is as if the Lord is speaking to me about something I had been dwelling on and just could not find peace about or a decision I had to make. The messages have helped me to put my all into Our Lord's hands and accept His Will in my life on a daily basis no matter what. I've never felt that way before. I always tried to handle things myself, getting so upset when it didn't work out. Now when it doesn't work out 'my way' I can let go so easily and accept that the Lord has other intentions for me and let Him guide me toward whatever that is.

Talk to Me about your feelings of discouragement and you will move through these periods safely and more comfortably. If you talk to Me, you will be better able to understand that your discouragement comes

from your humanity and not from heaven. In other words, feelings of discouragement are not accurate reflections of heaven's feelings about you, your service or your effectiveness. It could be that all is going perfectly with you from heaven's perspective, and yet, you are unaware of this for many reasons.
~Jesus, Monthly Message, January 1, 2009

Margarita F., CA

In reading the messages, I am surprised that any of them are for anyone else's eyes but my own. One of my desires was to help disabled students. It flowed beautifully in God's holy and divine will to where I am now as a speech pathologist.

The Allegiance Prayer has completely changed my life and brought me to the point I am now. When I first found out about Anne's messages, I very anxiously and eagerly waited for them the first of the month. This was about 4 years ago. It wasn't until about a year after I began to read them that I started to say the Allegiance Prayer faithfully the first thing in the morning. I would open my eyes, and upon awakening, there was the Allegiance Prayer at my bedside. I began to say it, and then I noticed dramatic changes in my life.

I am a speech pathologist in a school district in San Francisco, CA. In 2004, I went to Guadalajara, Mexico, to visit my relatives as I have done every summer since I was ten months old. My aunt, who is a doctor, asked me if I would like to visit a home for children with cerebral palsy. She had taken a theology class with the founder of the home. I agreed and spent the summers of 2004 and 2005, in Guadalajara. However, when I arrived there, the children were not at the home as they had been dispersed to their summer foster homes. It wasn't until 2006 that I was able to actually walk into this home for children, who had been abandoned, found in garbage dumps, or on the streets.

When the door of the home was opened to me, I saw a beautiful child, a little girl named Conchita in a stroller. She had beautiful blue eyes. I desired to pick up·that child and to hold her and kiss her. I refrained because I knew it might not be appropriate. Then, I walked into the home and all the children of varying ages (some even in their 20's and 30's) were all lined up in wheelchairs along the wall. They had no way to communicate. I wasn't sure whether to go up to them or not. I was hesitant. I didn't expect to see a lot of children in wheelchairs lined up along a wall with no way to communicate. Being a speech pathologist, I knew I had to come back. I couldn't leave these children like this without a way to express what they wanted – their needs, their desires. At the same time, this was a home run by a religious order. I saw how the sisters held the children to their hearts, hugged them, and fed them. Some of the children were quite deformed in their faces. Some couldn't move at all. I wanted to be able to do as the nuns, but I felt I didn't have the sufficient love required as a Mother Teresa would. I asked Our Lord to work on me.

In 2006 into 2007, I felt I grew closer to the Lord and received the graces that I needed for those children. In summer 2007 I went back to the group home with two of my colleagues from the San Francisco Unified school district. When we arrived, most of the children had already been sent to their summer foster homes. Conchita had been sent to her summer home already, and I desperately wanted to see her again to hold her in my arms as I wasn't able to before. I asked permission from the founder to follow the little girl to her summer foster home. The three of us took a taxi for about an hour drive and found little Conchita and another little boy named Pio. They were living with a very poor family in a tiny brick home in a very impoverished area on the outskirts of Guadalajara. Both children were about two years old at the time. We did speech therapy with her and Pio. All the neighborhood children came out to see who we were. It was a beautiful experience.

My life began to change as I felt the Lord was truly directing my path to start an organization called Children of Mexico and to go back every year with speech pathologists and other people who would like to help these children at this particular orphanage. This is an ongoing project I will continue to do every summer and hopefully it will be a nonprofit someday. This was a completely unexpected path led by Our Lord to continue helping the children in Mexico.

(**Note:** Information on how you can help Children of Mexico in the Appendix).

Allegiance Prayer for Lay Apostles of Jesus Christ the Returning King:

Dear God in heaven, I pledge my allegiance to You. I give You my life, my work, and my heart. In turn, give me the grace of obeying Your every direction to the fullest possible extent. Amen.

Bonnie B., NJ

Each time I read a message, I feel that Jesus is speaking directly to me, that He knows me, knows my struggles, knows my concern for my loved ones, especially my husband and children. I receive instant peace as Our Lord explains the importance of trusting Him and teaches exactly how to do it. I cling to the comfort He offers when He tells us that He knows we are concerned about family members and that He, too, loves them. I've had a personal relationship with Jesus for 25+ years, but this apostolate has helped it to deepen, mature, and continue to grow. When I read the messages from Our Lord, they confirm how I've always thought of Our Savior. He is so gentle and kind, even fatherly as He calls us "My child," or "little apostle."

You may assure each lay apostle that just as they concern themselves with My interests, I will concern Myself with theirs. They will be

71

placed in My Sacred Heart and I will defend and protect them. I will also pursue complete conversion of each of their loved ones.
~Volume Ten, page 46, Promise from Jesus to His lay apostles

Deanne R., LA

I thank the Lord for revealing His wonderful love to me at 7:00 am Mass on Tuesday, March 3, 2009, at St. Clement. During Deacon Frank's homily, I could feel an intense beam of sunlight shining down right on me as I sat in the pew. It was abnormally intense and hot for being indoors. Although there was no one else seated on either side of me, I didn't want to move away from the light. I wanted it to totally soak through me as I truly felt wrapped in His loving embrace. I had an overwhelming desire to praise and thank Him for His forgiveness and love. I decided then that I would go to the Adoration Chapel after Mass to praise and thank Him even more. So, when Mass ended, I proceeded out of my pew and walked across the church toward the Chapel.

As I was walking, an elderly man who had been in attendance with his wife stopped me. He tapped me on the arm and said, "Excuse me miss. The good Lord must love you very much! There was a bright beam of light shining directly on you during Mass. You were actually glowing! It was so beautiful! It only affected you, no one else." He was very emphatic. I looked at him, smiled and simply said, "yes, I know. I could feel that." Looking at me with delight in his eyes, he shook his head side to side, and said, "You are beautiful." I said, "thank you" and walked away to the Chapel with tears in my eyes. This man offered the affirmation of what I was feeling. I knew without a doubt that it was the Lord affirming His love for me. This time, there was to be no mistake, no confusion about the message.

What is most amazing about this encounter is in the days preceding this event I was seeking the reassurance of the Lord's love. I wanted a confirmation that in fact, He "had not changed His mind about me" as a lay apostle. His message from Anne on March 1st was His first attempt at this. The message I know was real. The Lord's love is real, all forgiving and all merciful. He wants us to give as much of ourselves to Him as possible; He is willing to take whatever we can give. If we do our best to walk in His ways, He will gently guide us – sometimes we may be aware of it, other times we may not. If we do not put forth the effort to reach Him, He simply doesn't have much to work within our lives. He is waiting for us to respond...

We all want that "beam of light" to shine upon us confirming what we already know deep in our hearts...God loves us. The messages Jesus is sending to us through Anne confirm this. For once in my life I TRUST Jesus and all of heaven and hold Them accountable for all Their promises in the Volumes! And... never once has He let me down and He is always there to pick me up when I falter.

Denise F., LA

Direction for Our Times has enhanced my life in so many ways. I know our Lord is speaking to each one individually in these messages. It has been 2 ½ years since our Lord called me to deeper prayer and Adoration. Through the mission He has brought me even deeper in His Sacred Heart! I use the Volumes every day of my life. My prayer begins around 3:30 am every morning until about 5:00 am. It has been the most fruitful and precious time I spend with our Lord. I have two Adoration hours because of this mission at 4:00 am. What a gift it has been for my life. In the constant struggle of the worldly pull on our children, He has sustained both myself and, through prayer, is bringing my husband closer. I live my life to bring the mission to others!

Michelle W.

I can personally attest to being greatly touched by the *Volumes* and other publications, such as *Climbing the Mountain*, *Mist of Mercy* and *Serving in Clarity*. They are inspiring treasures. Every day that I read a message (or messages--who can stop after just one?) is a day spent in greater awareness of God's presence and love. I truly feel as though each message is meant for me. When I read these beautiful words, I feel an increased longing for God in my soul that is so strong it is almost palpable. As a result, I have been spending more time in Adoration of the Holy Eucharist and at daily Mass. And even though my family has always prayed together, I have begun to encourage my children to offer their days and/or sufferings to Jesus.

We have also been praying the Chaplet of Divine Mercy together more frequently, although not daily yet as I would like. As one of my Spanish speaking friends says and as I frequently remind myself, "Poco a poco" (little by little)--a good mantra.

Due to my own spiritual inspiration and awakening, I have felt compelled to share these works with many of my friends and family members. As a result of my sharing with others, I have a short, personal story to relay:

One morning as I was getting ready for my day, I was talking out loud to Jesus and sharing my frustrations with Him. I felt let down because I had shared the *Volumes* with five other people over the previous week and had gotten little to no response from them. I felt as though I had failed and was sharing this frustration with the Lord. As I walked into our kitchen, I had a strong desire to read the Bible verse on my calendar. It was 2 Corinthians 4:1 and read "Therefore, since it is by God's mercy that we are engaged in this ministry, we do not lose heart."

God could not have spoken to me more loudly. I felt an immediate sense of calm regarding this mission to spread the messages. In fact, ever since then, I have not taken it personally if I think that someone has not responded to the *Volumes* as I think they should. I simply remind myself I am helping to "plant the seed" and that God will do the rest in His own time.

I struggle with the same thing once in a while. Recently, someone I sent *Volume One* to, when I asked if they started reading it yet, said, "Bonnie, this is your thing. Thanks for sending the book. I am happy for you. My faith is just fine." Sometimes it feels like a stab in the heart when others aren't excited to read messages Jesus Himself is sending to us! But, I have learned to be humble and draw comfort from these situations realizing they may pick up that book or CD some day, when their faith isn't "just fine." God's time, not mine...

~Bonnie

Rosemarie F., IL

Being a lay apostle is the best thing that ever happened to me. The rewards are so much greater than anything I've been involved in up to now. A more personal relationship with Jesus is the most important benefit, but there are countless others too: a more accepting attitude when it comes to bearing the crosses sent my way, a real joy when contemplating eternity rather than fearfulness, forgiving hurts easier, just to name a few. Never a day goes by that I don't read and re-read these beautiful, encouraging, consoling messages from Jesus, our Blessed Mother and the various saints.

Sharon L., PA

We have had monthly lay apostles prayer meetings for some time now. Whenever we have a discussion about something occurring in our lives or something we read the day before in Scripture, the words of Jesus through Anne address the very topic being discussed. We are always amazed - even though we shouldn't be. It helps us to see that we are either going in the right direction or need to change something. It makes us aware of how close Our Lord is at every moment. All we have to do is depend on Jesus more, wait for Him to guide us, and He does so without delay. Absolutely awesome experiences!

Victoria L., MD

I was not raised in the Catholic faith (or any faith really) and became Catholic in 1992 at the age of 35 – due to reading the purported messages of Our Lady at Medjugorje where I visited in October 1993. I have been a strong Catholic ever since, but as Our Lady said in a message from Medjugorje last year, "the way I take you is a way of difficulties, temptations and falls." And it certainly has been! I went through two divorces and a lifetime of serious sin, even after my conversion.

The Anne writings came to me through a friend about two years ago. Since then I have devoured them. I had become involved with a man after my second marriage ended. I knew it was wrong but could not extricate myself although I tried and went to Confession repeatedly. After two years of the relationship and several months of praying the "Allegiance Prayer," God gave me the grace to end the relationship and live a chaste life. It has not been easy. I consider it a "heroic sacrifice" and only God knows what I have been through – I did love this man.

I am still working on my second annulment. I have re-committed myself to my Faith. I do feel Jesus is reaching out to me personally through these writings. I feel called to be a lay apostle of Jesus Christ the Returning King. I have also joined a small lay Carmelite group in Emmitsburg, MD. I attend daily Mass and try to offer my sufferings up to the Lord for the conversion of other sinners. People may think I am a fanatic (like my children) but I know God is calling me. I certainly don't feel like I fit into this world very well. I know my true home is heaven.

Patty R.

The lay apostle books have changed my life and still continue to do so. They have brought me closer to God, Jesus and Blessed Mary. I feel the graces. I feel the relationship as if Jesus is right next to me talking on the couch (which is where I usually read). I now hear the voice of God the Father, Jesus, the Blessed Mother, and Our Lady of Guadalupe. I hear them from my soul. I talk with Jesus throughout the day and He guides my actions and words ever so peacefully and full of love. I long to be with Him. I long to do His will so that others see Him in me and are drawn to Him through His actions in me. I have had people say they see peace in me and ask me about issues in their lives. I respond with Jesus' words and tell them that I represent Jesus when I do "right" by Him. I then give them the lay apostle's books. I also journal when I read the books sometimes. Thoughts immediately come to me. What I write down are words spoken to me that are written more intelligently than I could ever write. They are Jesus' thoughts through me: His direction, His correction., His love and guidance.

It constantly amazes me how He does this. When I journal, I become much closer to Him. The depth of our relationship grows by leaps and bounds in such a small time. Instead of going to others with my problems, I go to Him. This is a huge change for me. I do not feel I need to go to other people. We work it out. He speaks to me and tells me what to do through the Bible and through the books. They draw me to the Bible as well. The books are truly transforming. Words cannot express my gratitude to God, Jesus, Blessed Mother, and the Saints. They bow down to our level to help us in all of our doings. It is total love that fills me completely.

Patty H., PA

This last message was impactful. We have a lot going on in our family (I have five children, ages 17 to 6). My husband is in medical training and it's been overwhelming. The other day, he came home and asked whether I had got this done or that done. He is a wonderful man. So I asked him to be a little patient with me as I am very overwhelmed. Twenty minutes later, I open my email and the monthly message says, "if you are feeling overwhelmed you're not relying on me."

God has a great sense of humor! This is a direct example of how closely He works. I feel 100% sure my relationship with Jesus has grown through the messages. God is so merciful, loving and forgiving. Every single month he keeps pulling us closer and closer to Him. He is wrapping His arms around us. We are all unique. We are all made in His image. We all struggle. But every struggle is different. The words hit us all. They keep bringing us back.

Sandi M., IL

Over the last twelve years I have researched the tenets of my faith, and have been very involved in Scripture Study classes. Spending time alone with our Lord in the Adoration chapel at my parish is vital to my faith. Anne's talk that day in February 2007, and then later as I read the *Volumes*, *Mist of Mercy*, *Serving in Clarity*, has brought a very vivid and real understanding of who I am to God; what my soul means to God; what I am to do to grow humbly in holiness for the Kingdom of God.. I give thanks to God with every heartbeat, every breath, every step, every blink for the GIFT of Faith that He has generously poured into my soul.

Trish H.

One late night in May 2008, while I was searching for religious books, the Lay Apostle website dropped down into my computer. I read from the website all night and into the early morning, and I knew God was calling me. If not for anything else, then to read for grace – and to note His need for more apostles. I wasn't shocked that God put the *Direction for Our Times* website in front of me. In 2007, God completed a doctoral dissertation through me on Spiritual Leadership. Between the attacks on my computer as well as reputation, home and family, I had to keep the computer anointed and ready for God's service at all times. God had to restore, resurrect and give me a new computer throughout the three years. I struggled to hear from God on how He wanted this piece of writing. Thus came the sudden drop down of the *DFOT* website. Extraordinary things become ordinary when God is involved and when He wants to accomplish His Will.

I have grown exponentially with each testimony I read and each lay apostle I meet. It is a privilege and grace God has granted this lowly sinner to understand the capacity of His love, no matter our past. Something I, and as I have learned, all of His creation, need to be reminded of daily.

Men

Independence is good in that you do not rely on other men. But you are designed to be reliant on your God.
~Volume Four, January 13, 2004, God the Father

I reveal Myself to you through these words and through the graces attached to them. If you read these words and sit in silence, you will begin to know Me. If you begin to know Me, truly, you will begin to love Me.
~Heaven Speaks to Those Who Don't Know Jesus
December 21, 2006, Jesus

Prior to my interview with Dr. Mark Miravalle, I googled him, and when I saw that his name triggered over 28,000 results, I began to panic a bit. I had never interviewed anyone for an article as I was new to the writing world. I examined his YouTube videos describing Mary, the Co-Redemptrix and his videos interviewing Anne. Who was I to be conversing with this brilliant professor from Franciscan University at Steubenville, one of the leading Mariologists in the world? I kept reminding myself God was at work here. With a smile on his face and hand extended, he walked in the room where I was waiting. I asked my questions, and he eloquently answered them. We had time to chat while waiting for Anne to join us. Dr. Miravalle is one of the kindest, most humble men I have ever met. ~Bonnie

Dr. Mark Miravalle, OH

My own encounter with these messages and *Volumes* is not one that honors me in any case. In fact, it's rather a dishonorable means in the sense that while I was in Milan and giving a talk to about a hundred priests, I went to the airport and there was a miscommunication with my assistant.

And as I got to the airport for a flight at 1:00 pm, (I got there around 11:00 am) the person attending to the tickets informed me the flight was not for today but for tomorrow, the next day. My ride was two hours away, the price of a 300 Euro taxi ride, and so I had no option but to stay in the airport. I cannot say I handled that news with joy and service. I was fortunate enough to find a Catholic chapel with the Eucharist in the Milan airport. So I went in feeling rather sorry for myself and this process. I was longing to get home to my wife and eight children. I looked into my briefcase and found four Volumes that the former Vatican ambassador, Ambassador Howard Dee from the Philippines had sent me four months earlier. They had been in there for four months. I simply couldn't get around to examining them. I'd been on some previous commissions of examination for private revelation. My sense was I am not interested in new messages. I'm not even living in the messages I know now. I looked down at them and I felt trapped by Our Lord now to look at them. I read the messages, and to cut to the quick, twenty-two hours later, in that same chapel, my only concern was that the flight might take off before I finished the *Volumes*. For me, it was a spiritual experience. I had my peace.

I started with *Volume Two,* which talked nothing about the externals, nothing about the means, only about our Eucharistic Jesus. I felt the burning of my heart knowing that this was supernatural. So, I had to be trapped by Our Lord to examine these *Volumes*. I hope that you don't have to be trapped by Our Lord to examine the *Volumes*. I hope that you can do it in a meritorious way because in fact there is an incredible food of spiritual life and thought in these messages.

> *Use My words, dear little apostles. Spread them everywhere. Keep your words limited and allow Me to claim the soul. You will soften the soul by loving the person. Your love and your example can predispose a soul so that I can find the opening I need. What joy is there in this work!*
>
> ~ Volume Ten, September 30, 2004, Jesus

The next testimony is from a man who shows me Christ's love with every word he speaks. He believed in me and my ideas for this book. He accepted taking phone calls from me when I was struggling and needed fatherly advice. And, hard to believe, he is my publisher! At the beginning of my writing career in 2007, I researched everything about what it took to write a nonfiction book. Quite frankly, the publishing world seemed like a scary place to be, full of rejection and greed. I prayed a lot. If Jesus wanted me to write, He needed to lead me in the right direction, quickly.

At the Eucharistic Day of Renewal in July 2008, I was introduced by Jane G (*DFOT*) to Jim, a towering man with God's peace in his eyes. I felt comfortable immediately as I pitched my ideas and wanted to shout for joy when he said he was interested. Interested! In me! I could hardly believe the path Our Lord placed before me. I promised I wouldn't fail Him. And with all the lay apostles He has surrounding me, failure is not an option.

~Bonnie

Jim Gilboy, IL

In October 2003, my journey began with Anne. I never thought I'd ever get involved with any locutions or visions except for Medjugorje.

I came from a very good Catholic family who always practiced their faith. I had three older brothers and a sister who died at the age of three. I married my wife, Mary Ellen, in 1960. Eventually we had six children, four girls and two boys. Then came the grandchildren, twenty as of today. In between the kids and grandkids, however, things weren't always great. I was in sales at the time and did a lot of entertaining. I began drinking heavily, although I had been a drinker in high school and college. In the early years of our marriage, my drinking was limited to parties on the weekend. My brother was an alcoholic and I had tried to help him over the years. I swore I would never do the things I saw him do while he was intoxicated. And yet, as time went on, I found myself following the same destructive pattern. At the time, I attended Mass every Sunday for the sake of the children without any devotion. My wife, on the other hand, had enough faith for the both of us. There is no doubt in my mind that with her daily prayers and masses she was the catalyst for the Lord to reenter my life.

1987 was a year I will never forget. I was sitting on the couch after my wife and children were off to school. I reached into my coat and took out a bottle and took about three belts of vodka, just to get my head going. I had bottles everywhere, even in my golf bag. The idea that I was an alcoholic never entered my mind, even though I was drinking at 8:30 am. I just sat there, planning to go to work, but I stood up and looked out the window and wondered, "Why can't I be normal, dear God? Please help me be normal!" I believe at that time the Lord jumped back into my life full force with His response, "Ask!"

But, my drinking problem didn't change right away. A year later in 1988, I hit rock bottom with my alcoholism. I entered a thirty-three day treatment center at the pleading of my family. And, it worked. In 1989 I was back to work and decided I needed to be working for myself, not for others. I started a business forms company working out of our home. One day my wife brought home a VHS tape from school from one of the women who had just come back from Medjugorje. I always wondered what it would have been like to have gone to Fatima before it was approved. As I watched this film with my family my heart actually began to pulsate, I could feel the heat it was so intense. I knew right at that moment I had to go there and soon. That day came in 1991. Our Lady ever so gently touched my heart with so much love, a love I have never experienced, but more importantly a deep desire to thank her in any way I could. That time did come.

By 1992 our business was doing great, and I remembered I had promised Our Lady that I would do whatever she asked of me. In 1995, a woman ask me to help her publish her book. She made it clear she had the money for printing, so with that knowledge I worked on it for almost a year before she told me she was in financial trouble and would not be able to pay for the publishing. So, my son-in-law, John Curtin, and I went to a small book publishing show, came home and followed what they told us to do. So now we are Publishers!

A very close friend, Sister Charla, a Sister of Mercy in Chicago, gave me a second book to publish. This was a huge financial undertaking and it was necessary for me to get some help, and, as is always the case, Our Lady led me to a wonderful Catholic business man by the name of John Gleason who made it possible to start our ministry of Catholic Publishing. In 1997, I published *The Messages of Medjugorje*. In 2002, two men came to me with a book called *Holy Hour of Reparation*. It had been first published in 1945. They asked if I would be interested in reprinting it, and of course I was.

In October of 2003, along came Anne, a lay apostle. I was asked by her friend, Jane Gomulka, if I would be interested in publishing her messages, and I flat out refused. Then Anne personally came from Ireland to meet with my wife and me. We had just received a new shipment of rosaries from Medjugorje which we sell at conferences, and I had recently put one on the Our Lady of Fatima statue in our home. Anne spent about and hour and a half with us. We felt very comfortable with her. I didn't commit to anything after our meeting. A week later, I was straightening up after the kids' visit and noticed that the rosary I'd put on the statue was off center. As I touched it, I realized it was all gold. It was a sign to me that Our Lady approved of Anne and I should accept her request to publish the messages. Anne began emailing me some of the messages from Our Lord and Our Lady through November and December. They were so powerful, and I truly believed they were valid; however, I still had some reservations. In early January 2004, I received a package from Anne with a message from Our Lord. "This contains twelve personal messages for the Holy Father." It was sealed. The instructions from Our Lord to Anne were, "Give these to Jim to give to the Holy Father personally. They are not to be shipped. I will open all the doors for this to take place." Well, it absolutely blew my mind. I called Archbishop Hannan and then Mark Forrest, whose wife's uncle is a bishop in Ireland. I also consulted with Cardinal George. All I heard was that the Holy Father was too sick and I'd never get this material to him.

At the St. Louis Marian Conference in January I met a wonderful woman by the name of Fran Dema and that was the beginning of the journey to the Holy Father. She knew a lady in Rome whose son was an altar boy for the Holy Father. Things began to move very fast. Our Lord said he would handle it, and so He did. We began making plans in February to go to Rome. Five of us including Fran and my wife, Jane Gomulka and Irena along with Sister Pius flew to Rome to meet with a close personal friend of the Holy Father.

We had the privilege of meeting the Holy Father's very close friend, and on Easter Sunday morning we met the Cardinal as he was leaving to have Easter dinner with John Paul II,. In the hands of the lovely Sisters going with the Cardinal were the personal messages packet and the first four *Volumes*. The following Wednesday at the outdoor audience, I had the honor of the Holy Father putting the sign of the cross on my forehead. Words were not necessary.

After two years, I returned full time to CMJ Marian Publishers to continue our ministry of selling powerful spiritual books, along with distributing the works given to Anne by Our Lord. People come to me for book recommendations, and I do not hesitate in pointing to the books by Anne. At conferences I tell those who have doubts, to take *Volume One* and *Volume Two*, go into adoration, and read only one or two messages, then sit and listen. In all these years I have not had one person come back to return the books.

The joy of serving is beyond words, the joy of seeing people who are coming home is even a bigger joy. Take the step into adoration with *Volume Two*, for He truly is calling.

I speak to you, My true servants. How I rely on you all. Each of you has a divine purpose and a role in the coming of My Kingdom.
~Jesus, Volume Ten, October 5, 2004

Driving to Loveland from Boulder was beautiful. With my computer generated driving directions, I headed to my first meeting with a group of lay apostles outside of my own in Fort Myers. I pulled into the driveway, the home of Ralph and Frances, to see an older gentleman with a wide grin on his face. A lay apostle... you can spot one a mile away. As Ralph greeted me, I was drawn to him, to his gentle manner. Then came the smiling, welcoming face of his wife. The next four hours we spent together was the beginning of a lifelong friendship. Their love and respect for each other is exactly what Jesus talks about in Volume Six. Ralph reminds me of what St. Joseph must have been like. His testimony is just as warm as he is. ~Bonnie

Ralph L., CO

For many years I have been involved in volunteer work and various ministries in the Church. I prayed, read the scriptures, and learned about the Father, Jesus, the Holy Spirit and the Blessed Mother but They have always seemed distant. I knew that They loved me very much but I didn't feel the love for Them that I thought I should, like the love I feel for my wife, children and family.

I prayed many times over the recent years that I would grow closer to Jesus each day. Then, in January 2006, when Sister Charla told Fran about the "Anne" books, we bought a set and I started reading them. I really got excited because Jesus was talking to me, not just the whole world but to me. He really loves me. He wants me to be His apostle. He wants me to grow in holiness so that He can use me to bring souls back to the Kingdom.

When I read in the Scriptures that we are to tell the whole world about Jesus, it scared me. I felt I couldn't do that. But through Anne, He tells me how and what He wants me to do to bring souls back to Him. First, I spend time with Him in prayer and silence. He is with me all the time. He never leaves me. If I am aware of His presence He will tell me what to say to people. Maybe a few words about Jesus or about how the *Volumes* have changed my life, or maybe offer them a *Volume*. That may be all I have to say or do. Jesus will do the rest.

I have been blessed by the Father. In the Old Testament the Father sounds rather stern. It says the beginning of wisdom is fear of the Lord. In *Volume Three,* He sounds like a loving Father. He says, "I prefer My children to serve Me from motives of love and loyalty." He also says if we tell Him, from our hearts, that we would like to know Him better, we will become His intimate friend. (It doesn't get any better than that.) He wants us to trust Him and put Him in first place. He wants us to ask Him for everything we need. He says in *Volume Four*, "I use each one of you to bring Me and present Me to others."

I am so blessed our Father is having our Blessed Mother and some of the saints talk to us. They give us such good advice and tell us that we can come to them for assistance, and they will intercede for us and send us the graces we need.

The monthly messages are great, also. Jesus teaches us like I think He taught the original twelve.

> *Your wife and children must come first. You are to lead your family to heaven. In heaven, the first will be last. Consider yourself a servant to your family.*
> ~Volume Six, June 16, 2004, St. Joseph Speaks to Fathers

As I began receiving testimonies, there were quite a few lay apostles requesting telephone interviews. One of those emails was from Louie. He didn't send his telephone number for me to conduct the interview, so I emailed him. He responded back the same day. This man is full of Christ's Love and Spirit; you can hear it in his voice. He calls me every once in a while to discuss current political happenings and how to survive the turmoil with Christ by our side. Knowing there is a growing number of lay apostles like him out there makes the craziness of the world seem calmer and gives me hope. ~Bonnie

Louie K., WA

I am a Catholic but lost my way for about 40 years. I was all business with no time for our Savior. Four years ago I went through a rebirth. My dear friend Larry has helped the journey in rebuilding my spiritual life with my Savior Jesus Christ. About a year ago, Larry introduced my wife and me to Anne and her very special gift to the world. Now my day is filled with loving our Savior and thanking Him for His perfect sacrifice. He has always chosen us. The question is whether each soul understands His Love and will return to Him with unconditional love and devotion. I fall more in love with Jesus with every breath I take. My rebirth is the greatest gift I could ever receive. Anne's writings carry the promise and inspiration that come with the pure Truth of the words of Jesus and the heavenly family. I share Anne's wonderful gifts with anyone and everyone I come in contact with. I truly have a tremendous love and devotion to our Savior and with every breath of my remaining life share Anne's messages of love, mercy and Our Savior's perfect promise never to abandon us.

Serve during this time of calm. Spread our words. Offer encouragement to souls who are seeking Truth. Bring Truth to souls who are discouraged in the world and do not know to seek Truth. Commit yourselves to Christ and let nothing stop you from His service.
~Volume Seven, July 13, 2004, St. Gertrude

Artur J., IL

My name is Artur, and I am 38. I grew up in Poland where Catholicism is common but sometimes more traditional than alive. I live now with my wife in Burbank, Illinois. I found out about Anne's messages with the help of my friend Barbara who already was touched by the messages sent and written by Anne in 2007. In the beginning I was a skeptic because I wasn't sure it was really Jesus talking. Meanwhile in 2008 Anne visited Justice, and my wife and I went to see her and to listen to her stories. She touched me straight to the heart, and we purchased books and booklets immediately before she even finished the lectures. Anne reminds me of St. Faustina Kowalska who also received messages from Jesus in the early 20th century. The messages are very personal and when reading them I feel like Jesus Christ is talking directly to me. I accompanied my wife through some life's changes: school, jobs, immigration, future, babies. Jesus' words really encourage me. I like the books about Heaven, and Purgatory too. They make sense in our everyday struggling, it is helpful knowing that the saints are helping us to get to heaven and become saints.

> *My friends, we are trying to encourage you to live for Jesus and His holy will. Many are doing this beautifully and you are seeing how He works through you. This is the encouragement that fuels further cooperation, of course. Be steadfast now.*
> ~Volume Seven, July 20, 2004, St. Julie

E. Ramos, Philippines

The day began like most other days in September 2006. I took my usual early morning walk and then did some work at home. After lunch, however, I suddenly felt feverish. By early evening, my fever had risen to over 40 degrees C, and I was shivering uncontrollably. I also felt a burning sensation whenever I passed urine. That was when I asked my wife to bring me to our community clinic.

The doctor at the clinic prescribed a broad-spectrum antibiotic to treat whatever infection I had acquired. My condition improved after I started taking medication, but only for a short time. In less than a week, my high-grade fever returned, and there was blood in my urine. This time, upon the recommendation of a friend, I decided to consult a specialist who's the head of the hospital's Urology Department.

The urologist performed a DRE (digital rectal exam), and detected an enlarged prostate. He then recommended I undergo a blood test to determine the amount of PSA (prostate specific antigen) in my blood. I went to a lab for the required PSA test and then went home to research the internet about the subject.

I was very much alarmed then when I received the results of my PSA test the following day- it showed I had an increased PSA level of 14.7ng/ml. When I brought the test results to my doctor, he immediately suggested doing a biopsy. Before I could agree to this invasive procedure, I remembered that Anne the lay apostle was due to visit Manila in November to speak at a conference called, "A Day of Eucharistic Renewal," and a Eucharistic Celebration and Healing Service would follow this. I asked my doctor to give me some more time to decide.

The days between my learning of the test result and Anne's arrival were filled with an odd mixture of anxiety and hope, fear and trust, denial and acceptance, doubt and faith. Many nights I lay awake thinking the worst, especially of how it would affect my family, but then, at the end, I just left everything to God in prayer.

The day of the conference, Nov. 19, 2006, held at the PICC, finally came. In the morning of the conference, Anne spoke about the rescue mission of Jesus Christ the Returning King, and His call for us to walk the path of obedience and holiness. At 2 pm, there was a Mass with his Eminence, Gaudencio Cardinal Rosales, as the main celebrant. My daughter and I played with the Bahay Maria Children's Choir during the Mass. After Mass, there was an hour Healing Service. During this time, I remember just kneeling in one corner of the hall with my eyes closed while Cardinal Rosales and Anne blessed and prayed for everyone in need of healing. What I will never forget was the smell of incense as they walked past me, for at that particular moment, I felt that the incense melted all my fears, worries and anxieties as they were lifted up to God. At that moment, I truly felt something special inside me had happened.

Three days after this experience, I went to the same lab to have another PSA test taken. I got the result the following day and it showed a PSA level of 1.5ng/ml, well within the normal range! My doctor was both amazed and happy to learn of the result. When I narrated to him about my healing encounter with Anne a lay apostle, he said, "I can believe that."

I, too, will always carry in my heart the belief that the Lord, through His servant Anne, had truly healed me. He healed my body of its ailment, and my spirit of its useless doubts and fears. In gratitude, I will endeavor to live my life in silent service to others.

> *Everything is possible for Me. I can heal you and cure you in an instant if you will let Me. Ask Me, dear child.*
> ~Volume Four, February 16, 2004, Jesus

True love of God and each other at its finest... ~Bonnie

Sean H., Ireland

My name is Sean, and I am 61 years of age. I married Liz in 1972. She was the same age as me. We had a beautiful daughter Seana who was taken to heaven in 1975 at two years of age. We then had a lovely little son Kieran who was taken to heaven in 1977 at the age of one year.

Liz had a very strong faith. Through unconditional love and example she helped me through many years of darkness, questioning and anger. Liz lost her older sister, father, older brother and mother in the subsequent years. All who met Liz would comment on the peace of mind and joy she appeared to engender in all she met.

I retired at the end of 2005. I had worked in manufacturing management in the computer industry in Dublin most of my career. Upon my retirement, we moved to Rathvilly, Co. Carlow close to Liz's hometown on my retirement. We enjoyed a very peaceful and relaxed two years.

In April 2008 Liz was diagnosed with cancer of the kidney. Her left kidney was removed, but the cancer had spread to her lungs and stomach. She was on chemotherapy and in and out of Tallaght hospital all summer. By November we knew it was terminal.

Heavenly Healing

We had visited Our Lady's Shrine in Knock in late summer. This was a favorite and special location where Liz would take her family over the years when tragedy impacted any of them. Knock Shrine has a wonderful religious bookstore. I would always pick up a book or two I had been looking for whenever we visited. We had been reading a monthly magazine, which is published and distributed by a local Catholic priest called the Curate's Diary. Every month he includes the latest monthly message to Anne. We had been reading the messages without knowing much of the background. Checking on the internet I had noted the title of Anne's books and had it on my list to purchase one. I purchased *Mist of Mercy,* in Knock. I had just started to read it when we first realized the cancer was terminal, and death was fairly imminent.

Partly due to our early life tragedies, we were exceptionally close as a couple. When anything serious impacted us, we closed ranks and dealt with it almost exclusively together. Liz generally did not share her woes with others. When Liz was hospitalized, I was staying with her 24/7. We had a private room, and the hospital provided me a fold up bed for nights. I was almost at a loss on how to manage our conversations. What conversations do you have when death is suddenly imminent? There is nothing about this material world worth talking about, especially if your children and parents are already in heaven. We had discussed spiritual matters all the time over the years. We did not have any agreed construct on how we envisaged heaven, hell or purgatory. By this time Liz could not read very much. I started to read to her sections of *Mist of Mercy;* in particular Anne' s descriptions of heaven, hell and purgatory.

I cannot put into words how much this helped us both. We started conversations on envisaging how it might be. I was pretty comfortable Liz would make heaven straight away; Liz had no fear of hell, but felt with the mercy of Jesus and the support of her children she could probably make it into what Anne might describe as the top half of purgatory. For Liz this would be fine. From Anne's description our children and parents and her older brother and sister could come and visit and support her from heaven. Liz's father and older sister were very quiet and conservative. Her mother and older brother were very outgoing with great hearty laughs, who within five minutes in a room full of strangers would have half the room in peals of laughter.

We created constructs/conversations for Liz's family and mine when they came to visit/say goodbyes about how Liz's father and older sister might chide her mother and older brother on their laughter and noise levels as they came to welcome Liz. We discussed what St. Peter might say about this laughter and noise as they were re-entering heaven? Everyone who came to visit would say that Liz left them walking out with peace and joy in their hearts because that is what they had experienced in Liz. Liz went to heaven on December 18th. One of Liz's favorite prayers was the rosary. In the last days I would say it, and Liz would follow sometimes verbally and sometimes mentally. In the last hour Liz was not responding verbally to my conversation. As I said the rosary, she would still follow verbally (in a barely audible mumble).

With Liz's faith she probably could have managed some of this, I am not sure. For me I was almost at a total loss at the time Liz needed me the most. I found with the support of the *Mist of Mercy*, I could do for Liz some of what she had done for me in earlier years. I will thank Jesus for this grace every day until the day I die and I hope forever after.

> *Be at peace, little souls of the world. Your God cherishes you and will care for you tenderly and mercifully when you arrive home from your time of exile.*
> ~Mist of Mercy, pg. 148, Jesus

Bernie M.

I just wanted to tell you that I find the messages really encouraging. I've been praying for spiritual growth in our parish for years. When I read the message that said, "Be at peace. Rejoice. I am with you and My plan is advancing," I felt like it was spoken directly to me regarding the prayer for our church. It gave me peace and hope. It was also a good reminder that God is at work even when it is not obvious to us that progress is being made. I wrote it down and put it on my cupboard door. A month or so later I had a trial in my life and this again was a good reminder to me to trust God, He's there at work.

John J. R.

I deeply appreciate all that I have gained from *Direction For Our Times*. The boldness which Jesus wants us to pray almost astounds me and is very comforting. I often felt that God, being who He is, would want us to pray that way, especially after reading the lives and prayers of many of the saints. But in the darkness that can pervade along with our brokenness, it appeared presumptuous. In our weekly prayer group we each feel that Jesus is directly speaking to each of us through the messages. We each have our own experiences yet each monthly message is like He is speaking it uniquely for each.

A little of my testimonial: I have a lot of business responsibilities that charge me up as well as drain me to exhaustion because of commitments beyond me. It is often 24/7 as they say. Things that shouldn't, too often gnaw at me. I constantly turn to these readings to find a much-needed oasis of peace, comfort and direction. They provide the insight I am looking for at that dark moment. They are direct access. When I awaken often during the night and my mind is racing, the gentleness of Jesus enters and I can rest even if I do not fall back to sleep. I have read all the books and *Volumes* and can randomly take any passage from any message, *Volume* or book close by and it is like being given an open door to the quiet presence of Jesus with the immediacy of now. Even as I write this, He in His fullness is here. I know that the scriptures, daily Mass, Sacraments, and weekly Adoration have a power beyond our comprehension here in time and God is very much at work but takes on added "nowness" so to speak. And the locutions through Anne are very personal, immediate and full of understanding.

He doesn't talk to me in the way of locutions, but He is there moving things, changing things, often very obviously, and it is not because of how something was said or done, but simply that He was asked into the situation. Those fully aware of the sudden positive change, where everything seemed to be going wrong, cannot believe the permanent deep change in persons they didn't think could change. Before I open the door to enter my business when I happen to know that there is a lot of turmoil building beyond that door about things a lot bigger that I can hope to resolve, I always hold the door for Jesus and let Him in first because He is able to deal with it much better than I can. I get to watch everything melt before my eyes, often in a very short time. I don't prepare anything; it is neat to observe that there is something occurring beyond human interaction.

I also love to ask Mary, all the angels and saints, to join in because they obviously have a lot of things they see from their vantage point that they would like to act on and can do so if someone in time asks them. I envision most of them to have tractor-trailer loads of graces from the Father, Jesus and Holy Spirit backed up waiting because no one is asking them for these graces. Another good way to see it is; all the power of heaven, the first string, is always lined up on the football field, but need us living in time, the second string, to hike the ball. Wow, what they can do.

Thanks to the Heavenly Father, Jesus, the Holy Spirit, Mary, all the angels and saints, Anne and all at *Direction for Our Times* for all that is coming into our times, good pertinent directions definitely, because we, while still in time, are learning we are to ask big. It is today's gift of our Returning King perceptively working one on one with each of us. Through His messages, He keeps me focused so I don't get lost and discouraged along the way.

John M.

The messages contained in the *Volumes* gave me new life in my Catholic religion. I have never been one to read a lot of books, so it was going to be, I thought, a real challenge to give undivided attention and to read them. Once I started, I was overwhelmed by the simplicity of the messages. God came to life for me. My prayer and actions have a deeper commitment on my part.

I feel more comfortable with prayer and knowing that God is listening, and wants us to seek Him out on all occasions, not just when we feel we need Him. I always felt and believed God was blessing our family, but I am now more than ever aware of the role He plays in our daily life. I feel the strength and graces from receiving daily communion and I'm humbled that God is so gracious by giving us the opportunity to receive Him. I must admit I was not as reverent in receiving Him as I now am. There was no quick fix; God has been and is still patient with me, but the continual encouragement to pick us up after a setback, and to ask God for continued help throughout the day restores us to His path for us.

Tom M.

I know Jesus, our Lord, along with being my big brother, is also my best friend. The monthly messages I receive from *Direction for Our Times* are just as if Jesus is talking directly to me. He is so gentle, kind and loving I can feel these messages are directly from Him. I share these messages with family and friends, and they share Jesus' words with prayer groups and all souls that need to hear from Him.

Thomas U.

Dear Jesus,

If someone were to ask me how much these messages meant to my life, I would not be able to tell them.

How much is a little distant ray of light worth in a sea of blackness; perhaps to a lost fisherman who is tossed around aimlessly by the waves? Everything! The fearful person finds a direction and his heart lights up. He looks up, and knows in what direction he has to row. He no longer looks down hopelessly but is animated beyond words. Yes, the ray is often obscured among the waves. But the first glimpse was unmistakable. And soon, it becomes more and more evident. The waves can no longer hide it. Instead, slowly they take on a glitter themselves.

This is what You did to me. Thank you, for the sake of all the souls who do not know You yet and who are lost, but are destined to You. May we call ourselves Your disciples, for their sake? Yes of course. It is our duty.

Orlan D., Philippines

I stumbled onto the *DFOT* website sometime in May 2006. I have no doubt in my heart that I was led to the site. I have been receiving the monthly message since June 2006. My testimony is not as spectacular as I imagine life changing occurrences happening to many who receive these messages. But I am excited, nevertheless, to share with anyone I can that reading these messages is like receiving a personal letter from the Lord Jesus every time. I am amazed every time with the "attention" the Lord is giving me. His messages actually address situations and conditions I find myself in at the moment of receiving the messages. In my joy, I share these letters with my family and friends as I receive them (I'm not consistent enough, though). I invite friends and family to visit the website to see for themselves and discover the joy as I have. I am praying everyday for the grace in my desire to do as my Master,

Jesus Christ, asks me to do, so that His Majesty may begin to be manifested in our world, in my smallness.

"You are here because He has led you to us. Welcome." *Direction for Our Times* **website home page**

Michael J. G., TX

I came across the *Volumes* in 2005. I had gone to an ACTS (Adoration, Community, Theology and Service) retreat for Catholic men when I came across *Volumes One* and *Two* and *Climbing the Mountain* (CTM). I skimmed through them but didn't buy the books. The following week I was at the Grotto of Our Lady of Lourdes. I went to their gift shop and saw CTM, *Volume One* and *Two*, again. This time I felt they were intended for me to buy and read, which I did. I started with the first two Volumes. After reading them, I went back and bought CTM and to see if they carried all the other *Volumes*, which they didn't. I went home and ordered them online from the *DFOT* website. Now I have read them all. I experience the presence of Jesus Christ while reading in the sense He was speaking to me like the lay apostle, Anne. They are strong and powerful words intended for everyone, but at that time, for myself. It has brought me a lot of peace, calmness, and strength. I've seen changes within my immediate family. I've been married for 18 years and have three children. I know and believe Jesus Christ promises us in the *Volumes* that in working for Him, He will take care of our families. I feel God wants me to continue in His work. I do advocating for children that are abused and neglected. I'm very active in CASA (Court Appointed Special Advocates). I'm a Eucharistic Minister at our parish. I was recently called to be a director for the ACTS team for this year, 2009. There have been a lot of blessings. But, I went through so much as a child. I had a very abusive father. Not only physically, but mentally, too. Adding to that, I grew up in a very poor part of town. Things were rough. I made many mistakes when I started dating and doing worldly things. But I know God has forgiven me for everything. And, I have forgiven my dad for things that happened.

Also, I have committed murder - murder in the way of abortions. It's a cross I have carried for a long time. I was also shot as a young adult. I was never able to forget about it, nor forgive the shooter. However, I feel the healing. I've learned to forgive, more than ever. Before I was very hardheaded, angry and unforgiving. When I see that God has forgiven me, I know I have to forgive other people.

I'm doing things now I never thought I would do in my life, like being a Eucharistic Minister in my parish, counseling people and praying for them. As they are speaking to me, I'm asking the Lord to work through me for them. I honestly felt I wasn't worthy due to many issues in my childhood. But I take it now as being humble and helping others.

I feel Jesus is telling me to spread the word of the *Volumes* and the image of Jesus Christ the Returning King. I know a lot of people believe in the Divine Mercy as I do. This apostolate is a continuation of spreading the word.

How powerful the testimonies of men can be. In a world where few take up the cross and lead their families to heaven, it is a breath of fresh air to know there are men in this world who aren't afraid to say they love Jesus. ~Bonnie

Youth/Young Adult

Through these young apostles I will flow powerful conversion graces to draw other young souls from darkness.
~Heaven Speaks to Young People, page 3, Jesus

Do you know of someone who is sad and struggling? Do you see pain or bitterness in your friends? Bring My words to them and I promise you that I will minister to their soul.
~Heaven Speaks to Young People, June 28, 2005, Jesus

Perhaps I have become more extroverted as a lay apostle. It comes with the territory. Once you consume the Volumes, the desire to spread the word becomes so intense, just as the fire of the Holy Spirit descended upon the first apostles on the first day of Pentecost. Isaiah 55:1,3 describes the feeling perfectly: "Come, everyone who is thirsty - here is water! Come, you that have no money - buy grain and eat! Come to me, and you will have life! I will make a lasting covenant with you." Sometimes as parents, we want our children to see the Light so desperately, we forget that our job is to plant the seeds, pray for them and teach by example. Sometimes, we think they aren't listening...~Bonnie

Taylor L., age 20, Boca Raton, FL

A few years ago, my boyfriend at the time, entered the Marine Corps. This required a lot of time apart; trust, and loyalty were needed on both ends. The first three months he was training in boot camp, we were not allowed to communicate, etc. I tried to stay busy and just kept falling apart, wondering if I were able to get through five more years of this. I felt really alone, and it didn't seem like anyone knew what I was going through. It was at this time my mom introduced me to the *Volumes*. At first, I didn't take them seriously, and I just set them aside. It wasn't until probably a year later that I turned to the books religiously. At that time, my boyfriend and I started to lose trust with each other, and the distance really got to us. So every time I struggled, I would pray to Jesus, and tell Him "through these *Volumes*, I need You to help me and tell me what to do about this situation. I can't handle this on my own." And every single time, I would select a random *Volume*, say my prayer, and flip to a random page. I kid you not, it always related directly to what I was dealing with. I knew Jesus and all the saints were with me every step of the way trying to guide me. That is why I believe this mission is so important. I truly believe this is Jesus' way of showing us He is here, He is REAL, and He will never leave our side, no matter what the case. I am only 20 years old, and I am so blessed my mom brought Anne's *Volumes* into my life, and hopefully I can do the same for my friends and family who are lost at sea. Thank you Jesus for making me a true believer.

I am returning to your world, and in this initial phase of My return I am returning through you. You should be joyful. If you are not joyful, you are spending too much time on worldly thinking. Think in terms of heaven and you will feel joy.
~Heaven Speaks to Young People, June 29, 2005, Jesus

Whitney L., age 23, Florida

I excitedly began opening presents of all shapes and sizes one Christmas, when I came to one that felt like books. Disappointed it wasn't the new shoes I wanted, I opened it up.

There lay a stack of eight little books, *"the Volumes."* I looked them over as my Mom explained what they were and how they had affected her life. A little overwhelmed, I placed them beside me amongst my other gifts. Once I got back home and unloaded my gifts, I placed the *Volumes* near my nightstand. My mom would talk on and off about the *Volumes* and how they helped her get through so many things and how they really opened her eyes and I just kept thinking I want that, but then after I hung up the phone it was back to the TV show I was watching. A couple months later, I noticed that little stack of books below my nightstand. I untied the stack and opened, *Volume One*. I began reading it with extreme comfort and ease. This lady had been through and done several things I've done and dealt with, the same emotions and thoughts and she was receiving messages from Jesus Christ. I couldn't put it down. Section after section I read until it was time to go to bed. I went to bed feeling almost lighter and then I prayed. I hadn't prayed before bed in a couple years. As a college student, I felt a sense of religiosity that I hadn't felt in a long time,. Then, back to everyday life I went, placing the books aside again. I would see the *Volumes* on my end table near my couch, but turn the TV on instead. Then, my mom called me and asked if I wanted to go to Chicago with her to go see Anne speak at a Eucharistic Day of Renewal. I was excited at the thought of a trip with just my mom, to a place I hadn't been, not really expecting what was to come. Anne began to speak, and everything she said made sense and really hit me that day. As she spoke, I began to get emotional letting some things go that I had been holding onto. She really made me place God in the center of my life again. I'm so ashamed to say I got so busy, I hadn't noticed I wasn't putting God first anymore. That day really changed how I am religiously. My mom and I were lucky enough to personally meet Anne later that day and when we looked into her eyes, she had this kindness that really made it feel you were looking at Jesus. It was surreal. My mom and I said good-bye and walked outside, and we both started crying. It was so amazing. Of course, I am nowhere near perfect, but I have made small changes in my life, thanks to the introduction to these messages and to Anne. I really must thank my Mom for leading me back to putting Jesus where He belongs: first.

> *As a young apostle in the world, you will have many choices to make. You must make them with My counsel. I have the answers for your questions, My beloved one. I have all of your answers. You must come to Me in prayer so that I can give them to you. I am your first counselor.*
> ~Heaven Speaks to Young People, June 29, 2005, Jesus

Mallorie M., grad student, Washington, DC

I received Anne's *Volumes* from my mother for Christmas one year, and just after reading *Volume One* - I was hooked! *Volume One* alone has accomplished what would have taken years on my own. It significantly enriched my relationship with Jesus; it began to "lift the veil" from over my eyes and helped me to get a better glimpse of Our Lord and His Love.

I feel so much closer to Jesus now and find myself having conversations with Him on a regular basis. Sometimes, when I'm in my car listening to the radio, I suddenly realize how distracted I've been all day and then, I turn off my radio and think of Jesus. I can really feel His presence every time I do that; I can feel Him smiling for remembering Him. He brings me such calm; and sometimes, he brings me to tears, because I am so overwhelmed by His Love. He is always with us and is never too busy to spend time with us, even if it is to share a quick moment together!

When I find myself in a situation where I am so frustrated that I'm at a loss for words or don't know how to react, I have learned to turn to Him and ask for His help. I can feel Him say, "be gentle, be patient, be calm, be loving." He brings me humility, He softens my heart and He opens my mind to others' perspectives.

From Anne's *Volumes*, I have also taken in some significant messages that have further strengthened my resolve, such as "Abortion is murder" - plain and simple...no "if's, ands or buts." Since my world happens to revolve around politics, I find myself dealing with very secular and anti-Christian views. Anne's messages from Jesus every month have provided me with the "fuel" necessary to keep standing up for my beliefs as a Christian, while also maintaining respect and being gentle with those who oppose my views, which is very difficult for me at times!

I have also come to better appreciate the saints and angels that surround us and root for us, here on earth. It is so comforting to know we have so much support down here! Anne's *Volumes* have also helped me to see the "bigger picture" and to realize my purpose in the fight between good and evil. I matter, and every act (big or small) matters!

The *Volumes,* and especially the monthly messages from Jesus help me to realize that my biggest problem is my need to appear calm and at peace, so that others can understand these gifts. I am naturally a high-stress person and become even worse when things do not go well. Hence, despite my relationship with Jesus being stronger than it was before, the perception of this fact may not be seen. We must remember that we are "ambassadors" for the Lord and have to keep this in mind in order to avoid appearing (whether true or not) hypocritical, not genuine, or not infused with God's Love. We must remember to always ACT like Christians, and not just think like them!

I have learned how going to Church can replenish the soul. I now yearn for Church, so that my soul can be greeted by the angels who can be found in the churches. However, my life is so busy right now (as it always will be though) that I have not been as good about going as I'd like to be. But this also contributes to how we are perceived by Christians and non-Christians alike: for example, just by going to get coffee before/after Mass and being seen in your clothes for Church, can really make an impression...whether it reminds a fellow Christian that they should try going to Mass more often, or contributes to the impression of the number of people who actually go to Church on Sundays. I always try to remind myself - given how much Anne prays and goes to Church, I can AT LEAST make time for Sundays! And I hope to go even more, since I have realized the importance and beauty of the Eucharist and Jesus' Sacred Heart.

A saint in heaven who has struggled with your struggles watches you closely, alert for a chance to assist you. They can obtain for you, through their prayers, a bit of clarity in a situation that is confusing you.
~Heaven Speaks to Young People, June 29, 2005, Jesus

James, MO

My name is James, and I am 23. I am a student at Webster University in St. Louis where I also work full time. I have been reading the *Volumes* delivered by Anne for two years, and they have brought me to Jesus in a way I believed reserved only for saints or existing only in the minds of Hollywood screenplay writers. In the short time that I have been studying the Volumes my life has changed in every facet possible. Physical, tangible changes began to happen to my body and mind; the people I interact with, my financial situation, and the jobs where I have been employed. I mention these gifts first only to say the physical graces I have received are truly the tip of the iceberg. I am eternally grateful for these physical changes and gifts in my life but still view them as transitory as they pale in comparison to the relationship I have developed with Christ, the Blessed Virgin, and the Saints through these *Volumes*. I view these physical changes as tools Christ gifted me with to do His work.

I am a sinner of course; that has not changed. Even before my mother introduced me to the *Volumes* I would not have considered myself evil or hell-bound in any way. I was, however, on autopilot. I use the term to convey that I was just living to work, eat, and pay my bills. I was lukewarm to issues like abortion and unaffected when someone used Christ's name in vain (something that grates on my ears and makes me cringe now). I would be insecure and take things personally while holding grudges and remaining embittered toward those that had hurt me. I felt little to no emotion when I saw others, like myself, who did not know Christ's love yet. I still struggle daily as I did before I knew Christ, but my struggles are yolked to Him now. I know there is nothing standing in my way that He will not remove for me. I move through my days with a confidence I have never known before. I move through my days talking with Christ. I am forever changed by the *Volumes* and I am forever grateful to God, Jesus, the Virgin Mary and forever grateful to Anne.

Children of the world, be consoled. Hardship during your time on earth is to be expected. Be peaceful about the difficulties that come your way. Look to Me for consolation. Tell Me your difficulties and I will comfort you in a way that defies human understanding.
~Volume Four, January 12, 2004, God the Father

The minute I finished reading the next testimony, Kristina became part of my daily prayers. Every feeling, every thought, echoed my young life and the struggles I dealt with growing up. I felt an instant connection to her. I only prayed someday I would be able to meet her in person and give her a big hug. About a week later, I met Judy, a lay apostle in Cape Coral to record her testimony. Judy takes groups to Medjugorje every March, and was leaving the week after we met. We agreed we would see each other again at the Magnificat meeting in a month. Judy spotted me at the meeting, so excited to tell me about what happened to her in Medjugorje. She began by telling me about three young people she met and became close to during her trip. Their last day together they had a present for her, one of the *Volumes* with a letter written inside from each of them to Judy. She became so excited as she listened to one young woman's testimony and since Judy and I had met the week before, suggested she send her testimony to me. The young girl said she already had...tears began falling down my cheeks. I asked, "was her name Kristina from Texas?" Judy's mouth dropped open and said, "YES!" We both cried and Judy could hardly wait to tell Kristina that I had been praying for her every day. A few days later, I received a telephone call..."Hi Bonnie. It's Kristina." We speak often now and Kristina has become an important part of my life. I am still waiting for that big hug... ~Bonnie

Kristina F., TX

My name is Kristina, and I am 23 years old. I cannot express to you how deeply I have been affected by Heaven's messages through Anne, especially Jesus', *Conversations From His Eucharistic Heart* in *Volume Two*.

Up until last year, I really did not know what unconditional love was like. Because I am the oldest child in a family that expected everything of me and seemed to dose out love only when I did things right, I honestly believed that I had to earn love. And since I couldn't ever seem to get things quite perfect enough, I felt myself to be unlovable. Every night, all throughout my childhood, I cried to God, asking Him why I was so alone and never worthy enough in my parents' eyes. To me, God was the big, mighty master of the universe who I knew cared about me and would help me someday. I spilled everything to God the Father, but I didn't understand Jesus and rarely spoke to Him.

Meanwhile, I continued trying to do everything right. I was home-schooled through a Catholic school, and my favorite subject was religion, so I knew my faith really well. Then I attended the University of Dallas, continuing to practice my faith, but I was an emotional disaster. All of those years of completely suppressing my feelings to protect and please my emotionally unstable mother, threw me nearly over the edge. I can see looking back that God really protected me during that time. But things seemed to get worse and worse. During my last year of college, I became quickly engaged to a man who suffered from depression and was emotionally and verbally abusive, while at the same time my parents began to go through a divorce and fell away from the Church. I was still living at home, so I was right in the middle of it all. Both parents tried to use me against the other, and all I wanted was to make peace and keep everyone together. But I failed, as I saw it, and I saw my family fall apart around me. I quit student teaching in order to take care of my troubled younger siblings when my mother left and my father rarely came home. I still balanced the rest of my college courses and a relationship that was tearing me down constantly. I can't remember one day during that year when I didn't break down and cry. It was the darkest time of my life, and I barely managed to hold onto the hope that God was going to pull me through it. I believed that if I tried to follow God's will and be the best big sister I could be, God would make things better soon.

At the end of that year, my fiancée and I broke off our engagement, and a month later I met a wonderful young Catholic man. Not too long after we started dating, he took me to a talk at St. Monica's parish in Dallas, TX, having to do with the apparitions at Medjugorje. Honestly, I don't remember much about that, but I do remember very clearly the man who came and spoke toward the end about a woman named Anne who was receiving messages from Heaven. He waved a red book up for us to see, and told us that he had read the entire book while waiting in an airport chapel, because he couldn't put it down. "Read this one first," he told us--*Volume Two; Conversations with the Eucharistic Heart of Jesus*. That stuck in my mind, and when my boyfriend bought me the whole set of *Volumes* that Christmas, I immediately picked up the red book.

That book showed me who Jesus is. I couldn't believe it. As I began to read, I felt my heart being wrapped up in a warmth and love that was so overwhelming I was almost overcome with happiness. Here was Jesus saying that I was important to Him, that He wanted to heal me and fill me up with love, just because I am His! I didn't have to do anything to earn this love; all I had to do was let Him love me. I cried every time I turned the page, and my mouth continued to drop open as I was again astonished at how much Jesus loves me.

Everything began to change from that point. I learned that I was created to be loved, and Jesus would fill me up and love me even if no one else did. And that made me want to love Him and everyone else around me even more. I began attending daily Mass, praying the rosary every day, and reading more spiritual books. As Jesus requested in His messages, I spent less time watching TV and listening to the radio so that I could enjoy the beauty of silence more. The result was that my life became so much simpler, beautiful, and serene. I found that I was smiling even when I wasn't aware of it. And people around me began to change! Somehow, I felt Jesus' love flowing through me when I talked to others, and they responded. A friend from work came up to me and said, "I want to become a Catholic, like you." My mother called me one day and asked me if I would let her pray the rosary with me every night. My dad read a book I gave him and began taking us all to family counseling. My sister, when she found out she was pregnant, told me, "I probably would have had an abortion, if it weren't for you. But I know you will be here for me."

And things just keep getting better---not because there aren't low points and suffering anymore, because there are. I've had losses since then, and sadness, and worry. But they give me the chance to run and throw myself in Jesus' arms, and He's always there to catch me. I lean against His heart and He tells me, "Be at peace now, My little soul. I am holding you tightly."

But not all in my life is good, you are thinking. I know that, My child. That is why you need Me. I can turn the pain, the anguish, the mistakes and grief, into strength, wisdom, patience, and joy.

~Volume Four, January 14, 2004, God the Father

I first met Andrew through Facebook. I joined his *DFOT* group and posted a message requesting testimonies. After receiving his testimony, I was blessed to meet this joyful, smart, and energetic lay apostle at the Eucharistic Day of Renewal June 2009 in Justice, Illinois. It warms my heart to see a young man so committed to Christ and His mission.~Bonnie

Andrew M., MI

I first heard about *Direction for Our Times*, the lay apostles, and Anne through one of my schoolmates, Patrick. I forget exactly how we had met, but we were good friends before he mentioned The *Volumes* to me. I remember that Patrick was always very adamant about the mission and The *Volumes*. If you ever needed to know anything that even remotely related to Anne or *Direction for Our Times*, Patrick was your guy. The first time he got around to mentioning them, I thought they were interesting, but they were always something that I was, "going to look into later."

It was somewhere in the first semester of my sophomore year of college, which would have been the 2006-2007 school year, when the messages of the *Volumes* hit me. It was when I was going through a trial and couldn't figure out what to do about it. It is something that is irrelevant now, but at the time it was causing me considerable distress. I was walking by the front desk of my dormitory while Patrick was talking about The Volumes to one of our mutual friends working behind the desk that day. I joined them, got into the conversation, and at some point Patrick invited me to read three passages from the *Volumes:* one from *Volume Four,* and two from *Volume Two.*

I was literally astounded to find that not only did the passages contain completely relevant solutions to my problem, but they were written as if Jesus Himself were speaking directly to me. I believe this was and is the most astounding part of the messages Anne brings from Heaven into the world: anyone may read these messages, but they speak and are completely relatable to the person who is reading them. It is an astounding and profound grace that is attached to words written in the messages that helped me with my problems then, countless problems since, and in my overall faith. Indeed, the messages have greatly expanded my faith life, guided me through rough patches, helped me further develop my relationship with God and Heaven, and gave me a better perspective and understanding about the truths of life and the world around me.

After reading the passages Patrick suggested, the fiery passion of the Holy Spirit was lit within me. I bought The *Volumes* as soon as I could get my hands on them and told anyone who would let me about this mysterious and glorious gift I had received. When the call came to form the lay apostles of Jesus Christ the Returning King prayer group, I worked with Patrick and two other schoolmates, Mai and Angi, in the establishment of a college lay apostle group on our campus. I was not as heavily involved with direct leadership as the other three at first, but when it came time for them to graduate (as they were all classmates and graduating at the same time), they asked me to co-lead the group with one of my classmates, Nicole, for my senior year. With Nicole's help and contact with Patrick and *Direction for Our Times*, we were able to further expand our foundation into the ministry of our campus and greatly increase the awareness of the Volumes and the mission of *Direction for Our Times*, Anne, and Heaven. It is now in the good hands of Nicole and my replacement, Teesie, who, I believe, will continue to expand the group and its permanence in the identity of our campus ministry

Before that, I had brought the *Volumes* to my local parish from back home, Our Lady Star of the Sea in Grosse Pointe Woods, to start another lay apostle group. I am also a member of Facebook and wished to join a group that related to the work of the lay apostles and *Direction for Our Times*. I noticed that no such group existed in any form, so I figured it might be a good idea to start one. I invited everyone I could, which didn't bring many at first. I believe it began with about 15-40 people. However, word spread and people found the site. At last count, there are now over 150 people that have joined the lay apostle Facebook group. After the group had been going for a while, I thought it'd be a good idea to start sending the monthly message to the members, which turned out to be a fantastic idea!

The *Volumes,* the monthly messages, Anne's work and the work of *Direction for Our Times* has forever changed me, my life, and those of the ones around me. I tell everyone I can about the lay apostles, the *Volumes*, and all the glorious things that *Direction for Our Times* does. I have heard and personally experienced many uplifting and heartening stories that resulted because of the blessings, graces and downright intervention of God through the words of these messages. I have been honored to have been able to be so involved with this movement and look forward to what is to come.

Another amazing young man... ~Bonnie

Tim W., age 23, Ft. Myers, FL

"Would you like to take a trip with me to Chicago in June?," was the only thing I heard my mother say; in reality it went more like this: "Would you like to take a trip with me to Chicago to attend the *Direction For Our Times* Eucharistic Day of Renewal in June?" Naturally I said yes, and having never visited the Windy City I jumped at the opportunity not exactly knowing why I was going. Little did I know that shortly after my trip, God would call upon me to spread the messages of *DFOT*.

The youth-focused portion came first on the agenda. I instantly connected with those discerning in Ireland and learned that people from my generation were actually interested in pursuing a life honoring God, thus instantly earning my admiration. It isn't easy to choose the path least traveled by my generation; however, I know my prayers for them will help in their discernment and that excites me. Knowing that you can actually help someone through prayer is a euphoric experience for me since it allows me to help others without physically being there. If more people knew the true power of prayer, more people could experience the same peace I feel every time I pray. With that mindset and motivation, I was determined to talk to anybody willing to listen about my experience at the 2009 Eucharistic Day of Renewal.

After coming home, I felt so full of life and grace than I've ever felt before. Listening to Anne and other lay apostles & speakers recreated the foundation to truly believe again in the word of God and how it lives in each of us. In December of 2008, I was part of the founding members of the men's group at our church called Leadership Disciples. It was my way to get involved with the church more than being a lector, and that had a very positive influence in my life as well. Upon my return to the group meeting the following Monday morning at 7:00 am, I

114

was eager to find a way to bring up my trip to the group. I didn't feel like an expert on the subject at all about *DFOT*, so I gave them the website to go see for themselves. Most of the men are retired and know more about tee times than technology, so they elected me to present the facts to them the following week. Typically public speaking isn't an issue or concern, but I felt rather insecure about explaining the subject to them. I came home to explain to my mother about the deadline I had for coming up with something to talk about for an entire hour. She was so excited to help me plan for the presentation, and the following week I delivered one of the best speeches I've ever had the privilege of giving, because it came from within, and not from a note card. The only copy of *Volume One* I had available I gave to a Pearl Harbor survivor, but everybody received a copy of the prayer card and additional information about the *Volumes* and booklets. There were about 15 men present that morning, and they were all eager to learn about something they had never heard of from their youngest group peer by at least 25 years. The men from Leadership Disciples gave me a round of applause; every single man came up to me and expressed how thankful they were to hear about this new movement in which they could instantly connect. A feeling we all shared collectively was the power of lay apostles like Anne and the effect they have on the church community. It gives us new spiritual life and renews our faith when we are presented with a movement like *DFOT*.

Terry S., PA

A couple of years ago, I was a CCD teacher. I would read some of the messages from the *Volumes* and the kids loved it. The students I taught come back to see me. They are now juniors in high school. I gave them some of the *Volumes* to read. One girl I believe is going to be a tremendous leader in the future. This girl is beautiful on the outside and inside. I believe God wants us to look like the world, but not act like the world.

So, she wants to start a youth lay apostle prayer group. These kids are devouring the books. The messages draw them in and get them excited about their faith. I actually have "purgatory" parties at my house. The kids were so afraid of dying. That's when I decided they needed to see Anne's video on *Mist of Mercy*. After seeing it, the kids felt prepared to go home (heaven), and all the fear has left them on death and dying. They see that Jesus is pure love and mercy.

Jacob M., Denver, CO

I'm Jacob and I'm 8 years old. I was in Adoration today and I saw Jesus at the Last Supper. And then I saw the garden, and then I saw Him when He died. Then He held out His hands to give me a rosary and a rose. The other day my grandma saw an angel blowing a horn, so I asked Jesus what that means. He said, "look it up in the bible." We (my grandma and I) have been looking in the bible and haven't found it yet. But we will.

(**Note**: Jacob's mother is raising him and his brother, Joseph, as lay apostles, after the tragic death of their father.)

Hayley K., Englewood, CO, age 14

Anne's book (*Volume One*) has changed my life by:
1. I have a closer relationship with God, Jesus, and Mary.
2. I have learned a lot about living by not being mean to anyone because they are God's children.
3. I believe in God, Jesus, and Mary so much more then I did a long time ago.
4. Anne's messages have inspired me to learn more about God, Jesus, and Mary.
5. My aunt and my mom have inspired me to read more of Anne's books (the *Volumes*).
6. Now that my mom has been reading Anne's book I pray every night.
7. I feel I am closer to God, Jesus, and Mary.
8. I am more thankful for my life.

At first I believed in God, but now since I have read Anne's book (*Volume One*) I feel that I have a very close relationship with Him. If I am hurt or in trouble, He is there to guide me to what's right. He always answers my prayers. If it wasn't for my aunt I don't know if I would ever have this close relationship with Him. Thanks to my auntie and thanks to mommy for taking time to read Anne's book to me.

You were created by God the Father and He created each one of you with the most careful thought. Indeed, in heaven's eyes, you are perfect. I am Jesus, and I am in heaven with the Father.

~Volume Six, Jesus Speaks to Children, June 21, 2004

Madalynn K., Englewood, CO, age 10

This book (*Volume One*) inspires me every night when my mom reads the Anne book to me. Ever since my mom has started reading this book to me, I feel a closer relationship to God. I had a rough start praying, not understanding how to pray, but now I pray every night always. I know that God is watching me from above and listening to my prayers.

It is important for you to know how to come to Me so I am going to tell you. When you wish to come to Me, Jesus, and tell Me about your problems, you must pray. There are many ways to pray and they are all perfect. One way to pray is to close your eyes and speak to Me silently in your head.

~Jesus Speaks to Children, Volume Six, June 21, 2004

PART TWO

Emotional Healing

Fear
Addictions
Tragedy
Anger
Denial
Depression

Fear

Also, do not be fearful. Why would you be? You are at risk of dying on each and every day you rise from your rest. What would be worse than death today would be for you to rise and not serve.
~Volume Seven, St. Gertrude

Faithful souls need to be told that fear is not going to help the situation and fear will make people respond in panic. What is necessary is calm, a trust that can only be achieved through a daily prayer regime.
~Volume Three, August 9, 2003, Blessed Mother

Anne D.

America has become a very scary place to live. *Direction For Our Times* has given me faith that Jesus still cares, the hope for a better tomorrow, and the love for everyone in my life. Whenever I feel discouraged, I begin to read one of Anne's books or watch one of the teaching videos on the website and immediately feel better! I could not get through these times without the messages from heaven given to Anne, a lay apostle.

In seeking the good of all of God's children, I must allow changes to come which will impact all of God's children. I do this to bring about the goodness and peace I refer to but the change will be gradual in terms of the benefits to come. Trust Me in everything.
~Jesus, Monthly Message, November 1, 2008

Patricia M.

I have been a practicing Catholic all my life. Since I have been receiving Anne's monthly messages, I have received emotional healing, I do not worry as much and I am not as fearful. I also feel as if Jesus is directly speaking to me through the messages. The messages have helped me to trust in Jesus no matter what happens in my life.

> *"I urgently needed Jesus to clear out the debris of a period of upset that had thrown me into the state of unruliness formerly mentioned. This is good to mention and I do so in obedience to the wishes of the Creator. It is good because we must all be fearless in the face of our weakness and propensity for sin."*
>
> ~Serving in Clarity , page 71, Anne, a lay apostle

Eileen F., IL

I was at a Catholic religious store about five or six years ago and a lady I know who owns the store said I had to read these books, the *Volumes*. I bought all of them. When I read the first one, Anne's story, it hit me in the heart. I read them all. One of my favorites is *Volume Nine, Angels*.

My son was in the army (he's out now). He did a mercy/security mission in Africa. He was there for nine months and then came back to his base, Ft. Knox in Kentucky. Then, he went to Iraq for 14 ½ months. Before he went I mailed him *Heaven Speaks to Soldiers*. I was hoping he would read it. I called him a couple days after I sent it. I asked if he was reading it and he said yes; it was really good for him. He was going to bring it with him to Iraq. He first got to Iraq in 2006, and that was when it was the worst time to be there. There were 100-150 of our soldiers getting killed every month from IED's (improvised explosive devices). He had been in at least 5 or 6 IED explosions that I know of and never got a scratch on him. I know this was because of Jesus protecting him. I give all the credit to Jesus, the Blessed Mother and St. Michael. My son loves St. Michael. I sent him to Iraq with rosary beads, holy water and the St. Michael medallion (which he put on his dog tags). He prayed the St. Joseph prayer a lot. It protects anyone who hears or says the prayer from all kinds of danger and from being overpowered by the enemy. He carried that prayer with him all the time. Every time he would "go outside the wire" he would say the St. Joseph prayer.

Jesus, through *DFOT* and Anne's books, protected him. I know it was the *Volumes*. I said the rosary every night. There were so many of them maimed or injured fighting for our freedom, and my son came back, all in one piece. We don't yet know if he will suffer from PTSD (post traumatic stress disorder). I ask him all the time if he's OK and he doesn't say anything. He doesn't complain, but I keep asking. Jesus answers prayers.

Sometimes on earth, My children find themselves faced with situations that I never intended for a soul. All heavenly grace is with you, I assure you. Here is what I am asking of you. Offer each day to Me. Pray for everyone you encounter in your day. Offer Me short prayers such as an act of sorrow if you are engaged in a battle where others are facing their deaths.

~Heaven Speaks to Soldiers, August 11, 2005, Jesus

Juli H.

I was able to give COMPLETE surrender of myself, including my death, to Jesus. Once I did, He healed my cancer. All He was waiting for was for me to be obedient to His call.

Take my hand and let me lead you. I do not want worldly fear to keep my children from reaching their rightful places in heaven.

~Volume One, June 25, 2003, Blessed Mother

Marty, Philippines

I'm married and a mother of five. I encountered *Direction For Our Times* the last quarter of 2005 when I was having problems with my husband and my eldest daughter. The desire to spread the messages from the *Volumes* was very intense. But my problems did not stop, and progressed all the more. Through it all, the *Volumes* strengthened me, lifted me up and gave me hope.

The following year 2006, my 17-year-old daughter got into shabu (methamphetamine), was gang raped and was brought into a rehabilitation center. Barely a month later, my husband had an illicit affair with his college friend. It lasted for almost a year. I contracted an STD because of it. It was a year of pain and suffering. But I remained in my faith. I forgave, let go of my anger and fear, and it would not have been easy were it not for the messages in the *Volumes*. I relied on Jesus' words and I tried my very best to live the messages.

God is indeed so good and gracious. In February 2007, my husband stopped seeing the other woman, and my daughter was home by October of that same year. We're all together now. My husband and I attended a Marriage Encounter Weekend last year. We still have problems, especially with my daughter. But my trust is in Jesus. I know in His own time my child will be healed completely.

I can completely erase your fear if you begin to trust Me in small things. Make many decisions during the day that you will not fear and offer those decisions to Me in the spirit of abandonment. You will see a change. Little by little you will develop a habit of trusting Me in all things.

~Volume One, June 25, 2003, Jesus

Barbara B.

I was married for 20 years. My husband left me and has nothing to do with either of our daughters whom I raised. I took care of my mother for 9 years. Feeling rejected, I made a promise to God that I would become Catholic. I did, but I did not follow the faith for a long time. I have had many trials in the last 20 years including a divorce, a daughter attempting suicide, a second daughter's serious sickness for five years, and bankruptcy. We almost lost our house last year due to fuel prices. My husband is a truck driver who owned his own 18-wheeler, but fuel was costing over $2,000.00 a week, and with his paychecks at zero amounts, we were forced to let the truck go.

When I met my second husband, we could not find a religion that suited both of us. I heard Anne speak and I felt called to follow. This has brought me back to the Catholic faith (I can't get enough). My marriage has been a little rocky, but we know God brought us together and we keep on trucking. Our finances are improving, but I always feel God beside me.

I have family who ask how I get through all of this. I guess knowing that if I do the right thing God will take care of me. I want to devote my time to helping whoever needs it. I want to be an apostle for Jesus. I don't fear things because I let Him do His job in protecting us and keeping us where He wants us to be. I guess I now understand the meaning of "let go and let God!" Thanks to Anne's inspiration, I will be a Catholic forever.

Do you trust Me, My child? Trust can be difficult, but this is one time when you can step out in complete trust and confidence because I will not let you fall. I am here, ready to save you.

~Volume Two, September 1, 2003, Jesus

125

Maire B., Ireland

I received *Climbing the Mountain* from my cousin Michael in March 2007. I registered with *DFOT* to receive the monthly letter from Jesus to Anne, and sent away for literature and *Mist of Mercy*.

How have I changed since then! I was afraid of dying until I read the *Volumes*, but now all my fear has gone. I believe Jesus will call me by name when I finally arrive there. I did have a personal relationship with Jesus in that I loved Him, as I knew Him from the Gospels, but I wasn't sure about His love for me. I felt so inadequate and unworthy of being loved by God. But since reading the literature and the monthly messages from Jesus, I have a much better understanding of Jesus' love for me and for every human being. He always says, "I love you." It's great to know He is always with me in every situation.

My faith has increased and I feel very valuable and loved. Every so often I look back on old letters and yesterday I re-read one from 2005 when Jesus tells us to avoid the world's teaching on comfort and ease and to be servants doing our best to help our neighbor and doing it for love of God. This gives me a renewed focus for apostleship and Jesus promises joy when we are working for Him.

As the books had helped me so much I bought extra copies and gave them to my parish priest and other associates. One of my friends is an apostle, and it is lovely to meet and share experiences. I look forward to the monthly message which I print, read and underline the parts that I feel are relevant to me. Sometimes when loved ones seem to be in trouble, I remind Our Lord of His promises to look after them.

I am always with you, dear apostles. You move through your days of service learning greater and greater lessons in holiness. I am

the teacher. When you offer Me your day, you pledge to remain with Me throughout it.
~Jesus, Monthly Message, January 1, 2008

Theresa M., NC

When I first started reading the *Volumes*, my husband George had just been diagnosed with lung cancer. It was difficult for me to concentrate on anything because of the tremendous worry, but I did after being prodded by my daughter-in-law. By the time I read the first four *Volumes*, I had an unquenchable thirst to continue with all the books Anne had written. My fear and worry of my husband's terrible disease turned into a peaceful "Trust in God" and "Live in the Moment" attitude. I felt strong and able to give him the support he needed to fight this evil with treatment that seemed would be almost too much to bear.

Because of the recommendations in Anne's books on how to be an apostle of Jesus Christ the Returning King, my husband and I frequently visited the Perpetual Adoration Chapel here at Belmont Abbey College. As a matter of fact, we stopped in the chapel for a few minutes on our way to almost every chemo or radiation treatment. The strength we received from Christ in His real presence in the Blessed Sacrament could only be described as a Divine gift. The adorers we met during our visits to the chapel were among the most prayerful, kind people we have ever met. They all passed on the word to pray for my husband and countless prayers and masses were offered up for him during this trying time.

I introduced the books by Anne to everyone I met, and I'm still in awe as to how they have affected all of them the same way they did me. The only way this can happen, in my opinion, is if the words come from heaven. The people I am talking about are holy souls who have a tremendous faith. We started a prayer group consisting of four people and are now up to fifteen at times.

We received graces from God that were almost unimaginable during George's illness because of all of the prayers and masses offered up for my husband. His treatments were very tolerable, and he continually commented that he was feeling fine and couldn't believe he wasn't affected in the usual way. The treatments were successful, but after a few months, the cancer was back, as expected with the type he had. His last few weeks were very peaceful and not without a miracle.

You see, in our humanity, we fear death and suffering. I understand this perfectly because I also experienced a dread of suffering. I did not fear death, though. I knew that death would bring liberation for Me in that I would be free of the constraints I experienced in my body. Dear beloved one, it will be a liberation for you, too. When your body ceases to live, your soul will become fully alive.

~Heaven Speaks To Those Who Are Dying
December 5, 2006, Jesus

Yolanda T., WA

I heard about Anne last summer through a friend who owns a bookstore that carries all of Anne's books, videos and CD's. He had personally gone to listen to Anne while in CA, and the Holy Spirit moved him to carry the messages she receives from Heaven here to Washington. I was thrilled to no end after I read book after book after book. The messages were filled with our Lord's pure love!

I had been a little fearful because of the signs of the times we live in and because several people were more into doom and gloom than anything else around me. When I read Anne's book, the fear totally left me and it was replaced with God's peace, love, trust and joy. I am no longer fearful thanks to our

Lord's message to me through Anne, His hidden faithful servant.

I am appealing to your heart and beg you to trust me and live my words. These are serious times, but I am with you and will quiet all of your fears. Be at peace now, and spend your time with Jesus in your heart.
~Volume One, July 2, 2003, Blessed Mother

Terrie K., CA

I want you to know that reading the *Volumes* and books by Anne, and watching the DVD's have changed my life from fear to hope. An example occurred during a recent fire in my hometown of Santa Barbara, California. We had days of evacuated folks staying with us, which was fine, but one night was especially bad. The smoke was very thick and the ash was falling like huge snowdrops. The windows and doors needed to be kept tightly shut and consequently it was 85 degrees inside at 10 pm. The phone rang every ten minutes or so until 2:30 am and with the worry and heat, we got very little sleep. I slept from 4:30 am – 6:30 am and awoke feeling unwell. I entertained the thought of not going to Mass and just hanging around the house feeling sorry for myself when I remembered something Anne had said on a DVD. She asked why John the Beloved was the only apostle to stay with Jesus and Mary at the foot of the Cross. The answer was because he "showed up" for duty that day and stayed at his post.

What a blessing Jesus gifted him with for his faithfulness - getting to take care of our dearest Blessed Mother for the rest of her life! I thought if John could do it, so could I. So I said my Allegiance prayer and "showed up" for Mass smiling and cheerful. It turned out to be a blessed day and I learned a good lesson.

I give thanks to God for this beautiful apostolate. It takes gloom and doom away from the forefront of the times in which we live and replaces it with true hope and optimism.

When you doubt, look to your duty and remain calm until I desire to erase your doubts. You will carry small crosses of fear and doubt at times, but that is, again, more practice, and these little exercises are good for your soul. Make small acts of faith to Me and the doubts will lose their power to distract you from My service during your days.
~Volume Two, September 1, 2003, Jesus

Anger

Speak with great love and gentleness and speak the truth. Often, hearing the truth will anger a soul. Remain calm and loving in the face of this anger and know that people were and are often angry with Me.

~Volume Two, August 29, 2003, Jesus

Truly, My just anger is abated by your humility and willingness. Do not be downhearted at the burdens you carry. You carry them for the Kingdom and each burden will win souls.

~Volume Ten, October 13, 2004, Jesus

Holly K., IN

I've been married for 6 years, going on 7 and I've had a lot of trouble with my mother-in-law. I think she has bipolar disorder, but I don't know for sure. It has placed a lot of strain on my marriage. We built a house across the road from her. I had been trying to tolerate her, but she is a difficult person to understand and get along with. But since I've been reading the Volumes, I started praying for forgiveness and understanding, so I can understand her and forgive her. I had a lot of bitterness in my heart toward her that affected other areas in my life. Just through prayer with God, He allowed me to forgive her. I had prayed about it for several weeks and all of the sudden the bitterness was totally gone. Now we have a great relationship; my husband is starting to come around to see her more often, and she's involved in my kids' lives. It's just been wonderful. The hardness in my heart is completely gone. I think the only way it happened was because I gave it to God. He lifted all that anger and resentment and the grudge I had and completely took it away.

> *You see, my friend, the path of bitterness leads in the opposite direction of where you must go. Come our way, to heaven, and you will have joy. The enemy seeks to divert you by encouraging you to persist in bitter self-righteousness and indignation. You know that it is not Jesus who advises you to hold on to anger. It is His enemy, who is also your enemy.*

~Heaven Speaks to Those Who Struggle to Forgive, page 7,
St. Faustina

To preface the following testimony, Cristina had married an abusive, powerful man while pregnant with their child. After the baby was born and with his connections and wealth, he took the child legally away from her after their divorce. The baby was 5 months old. The situation still continues years later. ~Bonnie

Cristina, NY

Now you know my background and the humiliation I have been going through for so many years.

I started searching for answers and for solutions because I didn't have the financial resources to fight the system. It came to the point where I was so desperate just to get justice out of it all. I drifted away from the Catholic Church, and I didn't even know it. Slowly I became interested in the New Age religion. I stopped going to Mass, and I started reading and going to all the New Age practices. But, it didn't change my life nor did it make it better. I had been reading articles about how New Age practices changes people's lives. I did all they said but it didn't do anything and I couldn't understand why. I remember always feeling that nagging voice in me saying, if, according to the New Age books you can do this and you can do that just with your mind, then where does God fit in here? Does it mean you don't need God anymore? Those thoughts always lingered in my mind. I became frustrated after trying the New Age thing for about a year. Nothing was working out, still. I met some people who were Christian, but not Catholic. They were Protestant and Pentecostal. They invited me to their church as I was looking for answers. They were very good people; they just didn't have Catholic beliefs. I began reading the Bible again and considering the Word of God through Scripture. I was very disappointed in the celebration of some Catholic Masses. When the priest proclaimed his sermon from the Gospel, it was like he was reading from a book. It had no depth. I questioned how to apply it in my day-to-day challenges. I couldn't relate to it. Going to the non-Catholic church did give me more understanding of the Bible. The people were great there, but the message just wore off. I was still searching for answers. Something was still missing in understanding God. Then, one day I had to go to court (in re: ex husband), and the judge and my ex-husband's lawyers deprived me of due process in court. They ruled against me without a hearing, which isn't legal. But they did it. It was an outrageous ruling that affected my life. I started watching Christian channels, but it still wasn't enough. I prayed, "I need to hear from you Lord. I wish I could hear Your voice in Your own words." I prayed for this over and over. I needed answers. I needed to know how to do things for the Lord, but I didn't know what that was. So, a few days later my mom called me (she is very Catholic) and said she was watching EWTN and saw Anne, and proceeded to tell me about her and the books. I felt like this may be the answer to my prayers to Jesus. I went to the website to order the books. When I read them it was like the most profound questions I had were answered! I was blown away. It was like Jesus was actually explaining to me and telling me everything I needed to know. All those questions I had hanging in the air were answered. The way the words were written, I knew there was no other

Christian book that was written this way and had to have come from God. The way the Volumes are written is beyond words how I feel. They are so simple, yet so profound. This started my healing. This was two years ago. Even though I was blown away from the *Volumes*, there were things at that time I was not prepared to do such as touching other peoples' lives. I wanted my own life touched first. I just couldn't think of touching other people. To be honest, I didn't have the desire to do so because I was in the pits and wanted out. But, slowly, as I started reading the *Volumes*, I don't know what happened. I started having the urge to want to bring people closer to God.

Rise each morning and do the work on your soul. That is always your first priority. Spend time in prayer. Be a close friend of Jesus Christ, not only in service, but also in communion of spirit. Then you will be certain that the work is His and not yours.
~Volume Seven, July 14, 2004, St. Damien

Mary K., CO

My life has become so calm and peaceful since I've joined the lay apostles. I can accept everything that happens in my life. I don't quarrel with anybody. With my husband, I take everything he is unhappy about and let it go. He comes around eventually. My kids are all wonderful. I can't tell you how beautiful my life has been. This prayer group is very important to me. I pray for them every day. I'm a better person in every way. I used to be critical of people – for example, they don't do their job right or why are they getting paid and not doing their duties? But now, I just accept it. It's them. It has nothing to do with me. I do my job well. I get along with them. It's the same with my family. I worry about each and every one. But, I've asked Our Lord to keep them in His heart and to keep them well and safe. And I know He's doing that.

You should remain calm and accept all in a spirit of holiness and humility. The times demand these extraordinary actions of heaven. There are many conversion powers attached to these words so see that you spread them to the best of your ability, following His lead and direction.

~Volume Seven, July 14, 2004, St. Damien

M.F.

Direction For Our Times helped me further the healing I know I needed. I have let go of anger and disbelief. I'm still working on negative behavior. But, at least when I fall, I get myself into the confessional.

Catherine B., MI

I came from a very traumatic marriage and divorce. There was domestic violence involved. The Lord has taken away all the anger. I am at peace and am able to deal with all that has happened with no hostility, no anger. It started with reading the *Volumes*. A friend of mine put one in my hand and after I read it, it took my breath away. A couple of hours after I read the first one, it hit me how blessed I was growing up. My uncle was a priest who had recently passed away. I realized how holy the time was that I spent with my grandmother and uncle. That realization hit me like a brick. That's when I went back to Confession. From there, the world opened up. I have also forgiven my ex-husband.

"Be calm. In fact, the greater the resistance, the greater is the necessity for calm. If you are not calm, take some time and get calm. Heaven has difficulty helping an apostle who is excited or angry. I speak from the greatest experience in this case. The enemy can damage God's goals if an apostle allows himself to be drawn into upset."

~Mist of Mercy, page 43, Anne, a lay apostle

Addiction

This is the time to let go of any habit that is pulling you away from Me and pulling you away from service to Me. Dear apostle, you must give Me your addiction. It can never be a good thing to be overly attached to something that dulls your ability to love.

~Heaven Speaks About Addiction, July 27, 2005, Jesus

You have looked after your own interests, either through the slavery of addiction or through the quest for worldly goods and sensual experiences...I am telling you now to stop. Stop any behavior that is separating you from Me.

~Volume Two, August 29, 2003, Jesus

Addiction has many faces... alcohol, drugs, pornography, even careers. ~Bonnie

Robert O., Ireland

I would like to briefly tell of my release from the addiction to alcohol. Although, I have always tried to live a good life, I never felt I was good enough or worthy enough. I was (although I wasn't aware at the time) an alcoholic and also felt the need to use drugs and often allowed myself to be entertained by pornography. I don't recall all the details fully; however, I do remember calling out to God, to Jesus and to Mary our Blessed Mother on many occasions for a very long period of time, asking for help. It was in the last year of my drinking that my sister gave me *Volume One,* of *Direction for*

Our Times, which I read, hungrily. All the while I continued to drink, but two weeks before my final drink I came across a Novena Prayer to St. Jude, which I began saying every morning for only about five days. I was lost. I felt destitute, useless, hopeless and very afraid of the way my life was going. I had no self-esteem. I disliked myself, resented my wife and my kids for nagging about my drinking and getting in the way of my drinking time - "my time".

My last drinking binge was on July 6, 2007. On July 7, 2007, my wife told me (for the 100th time) that she had had enough. This time by the grace of God, I was able to admit I had a problem and needed help. My life has changed so much since that time and although it has been hard, it has always been very rewarding. My relationship with Our Lord is getting stronger along with Our Lady - I am even talking to my Guardian Angel. I am an alcoholic. It is a disease. *Direction for Our Times* by the grace of God has shown me the way to accept and to trust in Jesus. I now frequent Alcoholic Anonymous regularly. I have made friends in this fellowship (I had none before) and my life with my family is a blessing. It is wonderful and I thank God for it every day. Slowly, healing is coming into my life and I am being given the grace to Let Go and Let God take control of my life. It is not always easy and I fall regularly, though not with drink, and I have been given the grace to keep going one day at a time. My home has become happier.

"We must accept that God's enemy wants only our destruction. The enemy of God has an agenda for us that includes unhappiness and eternal despair. The enemy sends temptation. When a person falls prey to a temptation and commits a sin or even merely an action that pulls the soul from goodness, the enemy exults. The enemy mocks humanity and works tirelessly to sow

*seeds of restlessness and anger, frustration and bitter-
ness. "*

~ Mist of Mercy, page 7, Anne, a lay apostle

Christine, NJ

I'm not sure how it started, or how it escalated, or why it
did. There are a thousand reasons, really. But, none so
significant that stands out as THE reason why I made work
such a huge priority in my ordinary little life. Work was my
drug of choice. Big company, big responsibility, and all the
bureaucratic nonsense that comes along with corporate America
-- the politics, the backstabbing, the camaraderie, the accolades,
the daily grind, the 10x10 laminate workspace, the morning
coffee.

I lived to work because it defined me. I suspect many
people feel like this, but I lived it. I found a way to use this
relentless drive to my advantage, and I quickly became a huge
asset to the corporate people who did matter in this artificial
business society that I lived in. But, I did so in a non-traditional
way. I didn't have the regular career path that would move me
efficiently through the corporate ladder like everyone else. And,
because my path was unique, it meant forgoing all the expected
perks that come with a traditional job well done – the increasing
salary, promotions and accolades that I felt I justly deserved. I
had earned all this, hadn't I? So where was it? And so
continued my relentless pursuit of getting these things, as I
struggled to get out of this eternal entry-level box that was the
wrong size. My workaholic ways came with a hefty price tag
over the years – all the long hours under harsh fluorescent
lighting, breathing recycled air, and trying so very hard to
complete the current oh-so-important task of the moment, all
the missed holidays and birthdays, my kid's first baseball home
run missed. You don't get any of that time back. I channeled
my energy into making everyone else look good, thinking that
this was the way to success. Surely, whomever I supported

138

would take me along through the ranks since I was so indispensable. I would be accepted, valued and validated. Or so I hoped.

But not all is bleak and gray. Something started happening in 2006. I had taken my first real vacation in five years that spring and it was wonderful. My darling husband and I went to the Caribbean, where the crystal blue ocean waters matched perfectly to the crystal blue diamonds in a beautiful ring he bought me there. He told me he got it so that I would always remember this moment and the color of the ocean. I felt I could breathe, as if I hadn't in many years. I had forgotten what that felt like; forgotten what sand felt like, and how the ocean smelled when the warm wind blew lazily across the beach. I wondered why work mattered so much. I was angry with myself for not putting life, family, and myself, first. I vowed to look at things differently when I got back home. I had so much to be grateful for, why spend it consumed in a vicious cycle of workplace politics? It seemed so empty, so pointless – so stupid. But, as I embraced the beginnings of what might turn my life around someday, I wasn't sure what actual direction to take to really get anywhere with these new stirrings and seedlings of change.

Later that summer, that direction was selected for me. Through some horrible circumstances, what had mattered to me so much for so long was taken away. They took my job. My work. My life. My very self. What defined me. And I was left alone. I wasn't fired, but rather "let go" because my job was suddenly rendered "irrelevant." That was the official reason when they told me. We all knew it wasn't true. But truth was far from the agenda this time around, so down the rabbit hole I went, with the ones I supported for so long nowhere to be found.

I spent the next few months running the whole gamut of emotion you'd expect when this kind of thing happens. On one especially pitiful day, one of my sisters called me and said that she had these books that helped her through a tough time in her life. She'd send them to me. I heard myself tell her that I would take a look, thinking that the last thing I want is some new-age religious stuff in my world – that kind of thing would never help me. Whatever! I was polite. I said the right things, but like an addict, the only thing that truly interested me was getting my job back. It consumed all my waking thoughts. If wanting it back were enough, I'd have never lost it in the first place.

Those books from my sister arrived on a nondescript day, in a nondescript way, stuffed in the mailbox. I opened them up and remember instantly judging that this just wasn't going to be my thing. My sister had told me all about Anne. I was intrigued, but the last thing I wanted was to get involved with was some fringe religious movement. I had to get a job after all – I've got a kid going to college in a few months with a huge tuition payment on the way. I have a mortgage. I have bills to pay NOW. Praying is all well and good, but it's not going to pay the piper, I thought.

I don't know how long I let those books sit on my coffee table. Maybe a few days. They had numbers on them – volume numbers. I guess you start with *Volume One*, I remember thinking. I didn't have anything better to do that day. Nobody is calling me back on a potential job. Nothing on TV except horrible daytime trashy shows. So, I picked it up and read about Anne and how she came to writing these words in the first place. Interesting! She seemed sincere and real, not freakish at all. I immediately liked who I perceived her to be. She had a gift for writing and making you want to keep reading her words. And, she's tied what she's doing back to the Church. The actual Catholic Church! I hadn't seen that kind of thing before. Better yet – she's not taking credit for "writing" these books at all. She's the instrument through which the words are coming. And, the words I'm reading are coming directly from the Divine! Now, I'm really intrigued. I was a Philosophy major in college years ago, and this stuff was right up my alley.

I kept on reading *Volume One*. I had seen some of the emailed "Messages" before. Seemed nice. But I didn't 'get it' back then because I wasn't ready. I wasn't meant to, but that day I was ready. As I began to read words from Jesus in *Volume One*, I got that feeling; that indescribable warmth that starts from somewhere inside; that you can't quite define or actually locate and just spreads to encircle you with peace, love, and comfort. You physically just bask in this bath of Heaven. How can mere words do this? I've read "holy" things before – got nothing like this in return. How is this happening? What exactly is happening?

What happened that day is that I was finally ready. What I wanted for so long was hitting me all-at-once. But, all those years I was looking in the wrong place to fill that huge void I had in my life. I was trying to fill it with corporate work, which is why it never went anywhere and even got worse. God is what needed to be in that void. God was that warm feeling. God was happening to me. Jesus reaching out. The Holy Spirit putting it all in perspective. Dearest Mother Mary praying so desperately for my little misguided soul to finally come around. All those wonderful saints that my parents had prayed to all these years and taught me about, looking at me. Those beautiful angels that had frantically tried to keep me safe and loved over the years despite my stupid life choices. They all happened in such beautiful rapidity and in such force, I wasn't sure how I could still fit in my living room with everyone so crowded in there with me!

I could feel them, all of them at that moment. Each and every one in Heaven. They all began to feed me. I was starving and had been for so long that I just sat there and slowly, but emphatically, and with such beautiful thankful grace, accepted their profound love into my soul. I am crying silently now as I write these words because I can't believe that God in His most indescribable love would have picked me to be the recipient of such graces. He made it possible for me to see what had always been with me – what was always there all this time. How could I ever deserve all this now? I had made such stupid choices in prioritizing my life.

We have seen and read accounts from throughout the ages of God reaching out to us, and they are all profound and amazing. But, these words in the *Volumes* are for us in our time, in our language. Written for us in this world right now. And, though timeless in nature, they are also timely in their subjectivity because any one message touches ALL of us no matter what path we're on in this life, or what cross we're struggling with. From that first day I picked up *Volume One*, my life has never been the same, and I thank God for that. I am different. I'm awake now. I'm fed. I have an acute awareness of the infinite possibility that lies ahead with this heavenly army that travels with me. I know what life priorities are supposed to look like now, I just wasn't able or ready to really see how wrong of a path I was on only a few short years ago.

More than two years have passed since that nondescript day that, unbeknownst to me, would change my life. That one little book ignited a proverbial fire in my soul and in many others as well. But, as all of you know, this is not just about a material "book." The actual book is only the doorbell to what awaits when you open your heart and let in the heavenly army who so desperately wants you. They have been waiting for you to look their way, and want so much to ask God to fill you up with the most wonderful graces you can imagine. Such things will not be found in the material world among our confines of space and time, and when we look for them there, we will not find them. We only need to gaze up to find Heaven looking back at us in reassurance that yes, they are all really there. God directs us all – Heaven and earth - and He would like us to help with His various plan details by adding our own unique contributions to His great tapestry. We only need to just say "yes" to Him to begin this process. The blessings that I, personally, have received are so many. I am humbled and awed at this heavenly family that surrounds me in such beautiful arms, and holds me so close. Within their embrace, I have learned to breathe again, and to sustain that breath, and to share with others the way they too can begin to breathe again. And, believe me, Heaven has patiently been waiting for me to come around for quite a while now! I thank God for this intervention because to go on as I had been would have continued a lonely, unfulfilled, empty life and a waste of a potential helper for Him here on earth. I went through a kind of Divine heavenly rehab and came out stronger and better for it. My heavenly education through the *Volumes* remains on-going and my struggles to consistently stay on course also remain.

"They were given the eyes to see their addiction, their selfishness, their sinfulness. They then got sober and became some of the greatest servants of Christ."
~Volume One, page 40, Anne, a lay apostle

Tragedy

My graces pour down upon you during these times. You must also ask yourself always what it is that Jesus is attempting to show you through tragedy or illness.
~Volume One, July 16, 2003, Jesus

My friend, there are events in every life that stand out as difficult and life-altering. This tragedy, this abrupt change of course, will stand out to you, I know. When you feel a sense of shock, a sense of stunning upset in your life, you must look for Me. I am there.
~ Heaven Speaks to Those Who Experience Tragedy ,
December 12, 2006, Jesus

Tragedy can strike at a moment's notice. When something unexpected occurs creating unimaginable outcomes, without knowledge of the Truth, our lives can spiral out of control. The following testimony is from a woman I was referred to by *DFOT*. My first conversation with Des was remarkable. Her story is one of true tragedy, unimaginable devastation. Meeting her in person, one would never know she experienced this great loss. She is joyful, filled with the Holy Spirit. Her story has profoundly affected how I perceive my life and the lives of my loved ones... ~Bonnie

Desiree M., Denver, CO

My husband Joseph was a good man so full of life and love. He would do anything to help another human being. He

144

was very devoted to Our Lady and loved Jesus with all of his heart and soul.

When I first met Joseph he was 19 years old and coming out of a deep depression. I was 18. I guess back then our prayers must have infused together and became one prayer because for over 20 years, he never showed signs of depression and had not needed antidepressants until the tragedy in 2007. I remember asking Joseph at one point what healed him after so many years of depression. He said he remembered crying out to the Lord back then to please heal him. He said the Lord put him in his life at that time and I loved him for him. The funny thing is, I remember crying out from the depths of my heart back then too, to please heal Joseph because I knew that he could become the man God created him to be. This is why I feel our prayers became infused as one.

In July of 2007 my husband was diagnosed with clinical depression. I will always remember the deep sadness and sorrow. He was put on an antidepressant medication and started taking it the fourth of July. He stayed home on July fifth. He said he needed to get some rest and that he still wasn't feeling very well from the depression. So I agreed with him to get some rest and stay home. I told him to call me at work if he needed me. He gave me a kiss and said he loved me. He gave our two sons a kiss on the forehead and said, "Goodbye, hijos. I love you." Little did I realize he was at the deepest low of depression. After I dropped my sons off at daycare, I remember crying all the way to work because I was so worried about him. I felt like my heart was in my stomach. It was a horrible feeling. When I arrived at work I called all of my prayer warriors over to my desk and told them I was worried about my husband because of his new diagnosis and that he stayed home because he was feeling sick. We lifted him up in prayer and all I could do was cry.

At 11:00 am. I tried to call him from work but there was no answer. I was frantic and feeling very uneasy. I called my mother and asked if she could keep calling and check on him because he was not answering the telephone, and I was very worried and concerned. She called but the phone rang and rang. She thought maybe he just went for a walk. I called the daycare where my sons were because our neighbor worked there and I knew she got off work every day at 1:00 pm. I asked her if she could check on Joe because he was sick at home and was not answering the telephone. She said she would check on him for me.

The day went by and it was time for me to leave and pick up the kids at daycare. I rushed out of the office and didn't say good-bye to anyone. According to my co-workers, I acted strange and wasn't my normal self.

I remember driving home praying everything would be fine and I would find my husband working on his artwork or taking a nap. When I got closer to home I distinctly heard my Guardian Angel say, "go home and check on Joe before picking up the boys." I said out loud I submit to Heaven with all obedience and I'd do whatever heaven would like for me to do. I turned down our street and saw that my husband's truck was parked in the drive way, the mail was still in the mailbox and our front door was closed shut which was unusual considering it was in the 70's. I just had this horrible feeling something bad must have happened. I never imagined what I found could ever happen to me.

I called out his name several times with no answer. Our dog was whimpering and crying. I went downstairs and thought the worst. I thought I would find him on the couch lying there from a heart attack or something. The light was on in the bathroom and I could tell he was going to take a shower because he had his belt and clean underwear hanging from the towel rack. The clothes he ironed that day were lying on top of the couch. Still there was no Joe. I yelled and called out for him but still no answer. He was nowhere to be found. I ran upstairs and out our back sliding doors. I yelled for him in the backyard and ran to the garage. I tried to open the door to the garage but it was locked. I knew right there and then something horrible happened because we never keep the door locked. My husband works on his artwork in the summertime out in the garage and we never lock the door. I ran inside and called my mom on the cordless phone and told her that I couldn't find Joe anywhere and that I was worried. She said again, maybe he just went for a walk. I told her the garage door was locked and I couldn't get in. She told me to calm down and get the keys and let myself into the garage. The strange thing is that I didn't see the keys hanging on the key rack but I knew where they were because a thought popped in my head to check the cabinet where we keep the medication. And sure enough I found the keys right by the bottle of his antidepressant medication.

My mother told me to keep her on the telephone. I did and proceeded to the garage door. There were about 15 keys on this key chain and I had no clue which key opened the garage door since they were not marked, and we never locked it. I couldn't believe it. The first key I tried opened the door. To my horrible unexpected terror, I saw my husband. He had hanged himself. It was so horrible; I felt as though my whole world had come crashing down and the life I knew had ended in an instant. I was beside myself. I was shocked and in disbelief. It felt like someone had stomped on my heart a million times, then shattering another billion times over and over again. I wanted to just run up to him and hug him by his legs. I told my mom it was so dark in there. How in the world could he have done this to himself? I didn't understand. I told her I couldn't go in there because it wasn't Joe anymore. It was an empty shell. He was gone now. I felt the presence of evil, and my Guardian Angel wouldn't allow me to go in. Mom told me not to go in there and to listen to my Guardian Angel. She told me to go next door to the neighbor's house to call 911. I remember saying, 'Joe where are you? Where is your soul? I can't find you...God where is he? Please, he was a good man. I love him. Why? Why did he have to die this way? No, no...why did you hang yourself Joe? I love you. My heart is so broken.' I remember reaching out looking for his soul. If I could have I would have curled up in a little ball and just lay there and died along with my husband. I remember dialing 911. The neighbors had to take the phone from me because I couldn't talk anymore. I was in a state of shock, reality and fantasy all at the same time. I was having thoughts that this couldn't be happening. Please let me wake-up from this horrible nightmare. I can't go on without my husband. What about our sons? What am I going to tell them? They are only 7 and 5 years old. God help me.' I was a total mess.

I was so close to my husband that it is hard for me to detach myself from him even though I know he made his journey home and is in heaven forever. I know that I will see him again because I feel so at peace while I am in deep prayer. My sons, Jacob and Joseph, are suffering so much because they miss their daddy. It breaks my heart. Jacob is 7, and Joe Jr. is 5. They don't know how their dad passed away. I am afraid it would break their little hearts. I told them daddy was very sick and the Lord took him home to heaven. I know in the future I will have to tell them the truth about depression. Who knows, maybe the Lord will come back by then, and he will spare me of telling them exactly what happened. The amazing thing in all of this is that Joseph went to church with us the Sunday before he passed away, even though he was feeling sick from the depression. He went to Confession and received the Eucharist.

It's been almost two years and I finally understand why my husband was such a loving, forgiving and kind person. He understood the meaning of living life with love and kindness. But on the inside he was silently struggling with his depression. My husband felt the loneliness, sadness, sorrow, and emptiness associated with the mental illness of depression. A person can be smiling on the outside, but still be wounded very deeply on the inside. It is very important for us to teach our children along with others and ourselves to be careful with words and actions.

A lot of damage can be done deep inside a heart if treated unkindly. We need to allow Jesus to radiate his beautiful love out of us.

I didn't know anything about Anne's messages from heaven until September of 2007, thanks to a good friend of mine Becky whom I met in Denver. She now lives in Norway, and her husband is translating the *Volumes* into Norwegian. She told me I should read the messages of Anne, a lay apostle and especially the book *Mist of Mercy*. I did and then the graces and blessings started. I have read all the *Volumes* and they have healed me immensely and I contribute my healing over the loss of my husband to these books, Mass, the lay apostle prayer group we started in Denver, attending Adoration and prayer at a healing Mass. My sons started having dreams about being with their daddy in Heaven and now have a desire to become priests. Before I got my hands on these beautiful messages I remember telling the boys we now work for the Kingdom of Heaven, and we are going to help save souls.

I had been hesitant to talk about my husband's suicide until I flew for the first time to a Eucharistic Day of Renewal in summer 2008. During the prayer conference I was given the grace of clarity. I was sitting talking to a couple, total strangers, and found myself giving my testimony. I told them how the messages have healed me and changed my life after the loss of my husband. I was talking about God's great love and mercy when all of a sudden I started to feel the Holy Spirit come over me. I told the couple I felt the Holy Spirit upon me, and I thanked them. By allowing me to share my story, I was liberated and set free. I am not afraid to share it with others anymore. I don't care what anyone thinks. It doesn't matter as long as I am letting go of self-will and allowing my dear, sweet Lord's will be done. I know I must reach out and help others left behind after a loved one commits suicide because of a mental illness. Jesus took away my fear since He knew I would worry about what others would think of me.

God's great love and mercy have allowed many graces and blessings to flow down from heaven upon many during this time. We are all so unworthy of these blessings and graces. But because we're open to receiving them and willing to share our testimonies to heal others, He has allowed it to happen. It can happen to anybody opening his or her heart to Jesus.

I pray that the Lord may heal the brokenness and wounded little hearts and make all families whole again, that they may experience joy, peace, calm and love that only heaven can give. This is what Jesus and Our Lady have done for my family. We are witnesses to how Jesus can heal if you surrender to Him and don't let go of Him no matter what tragedy is experienced. Trust in Jesus for He is the way and allow Our Lady to lead you by the hand to her Son Jesus and all will be well. I know this because He has made my two sons and me whole again and has healed us of our deep sadness, and without a doubt know one day we will be united with Him again in the Kingdom of Heaven. We give God all thanksgiving and glory...we sing praises and we will serve the Lord for all eternity.

A lovely woman sitting in front of my daughter Whitney and me at the Eucharistic Day of Renewal July 2008 was introduced to us as someone I needed to interview for a testimony. As she began to speak, reliving the tragedy she experienced, I couldn't comprehend her attitude. I couldn't believe her calm and accepting nature. She defines inspiration... ~Bonnie

Marilynn L., KY

I have been trying to find my way and purpose for a long time now. Then one day I opened a Queen of Peace newsletter standing at the counter at The Marian Center where I volunteer. I saw a two-page layout of Anne's *Volumes*. One of the pictures was Pope John Paul II receiving a set of the *Volumes*. I gasped, because someone from CMJ Marian Publishers approached me in the Spring of 2004, when I called in a book order for the store and asked if they could send me at that time five of the *Volumes* to read. They said that a woman named Anne was receiving messages from Jesus, Mary and the Saints. I asked if they had the Imprimatur and they responded no, but that they were seeking an Imprimatur and going to give Pope John Paul II a set of them. I asked them to send me the books. I would read them and present them to our President of the Center. I would get back with them when they had acquired the Imprimatur.

I read the books and was very taken with them, awaiting word of the Imprimatur. I placed them on my bookshelf and forgot about them. I almost gave them away when something told me to hold on to them. I'm sure it was my guardian angel. Then shortly after I saw the ad, I learned there were more *Volumes* added, and a book called *Climbing The Mountain*. So I got the books back out and began to read them again and ordered more for the store. Being very conservative and not sure they would sell, I only ordered a couple of sets. I didn't realize the domino effect it would have on all of our lives. The books have changed many lives especially mine.

After I had read the Volumes, *Climbing The Mountain* and *Mist of Mercy*, I knew the words I read were Real, a Truth. I truly knew they were directly from Jesus, Mary and the Saints. I was so excited about sharing what I had discovered. I gave a talk for our prayer group on two Monday nights at Guardian Angels Church. The response was overwhelming. Everyone wanted to order a set. So we ordered more. After reading the books I believed the promises that Jesus had made and I wanted to be a lay apostle and help Jesus win back his people. I began to recite the Allegiance Prayer every day. Then we started a lay apostle prayer group at The Marian Center. It had expanded, and we moved it to Guardian Angels Church with Adoration conducted by a priest. I too started a prayer group of my own. I found myself letting Jesus know that I not only wanted to help

Him win back His people, but I was willing to give my "yes" to Him and willing to work in any way that I could.

Little did I know that on Tuesday August 15, 2006, my life would change dramatically, forever. A friend and I were on our way home from The Marian Center to get ready for church for holy day, the feast of the Assumption. While sitting at a traffic light, a man in a truck speeding on the opposite side of the street clipped a car that turned in front of him. He went air-borne and landed upside down on top of my car. The impact severed off my left arm. When I awoke in the hospital I was filled with such peace and joy. It didn't make sense to those in the world nor myself, but I knew it had to be supernatural. It was nothing I could have manifested but instead a peace and joy only God could give. I have no anger or animosity toward anyone especially God. When I awoke, I responded by saying He gave His life for salvation, I only gave an arm. I gladly did it for His Glory. I only hope by offering my suffering I can help Him win back His people. I believe if I had not read

The *Volumes, Climbing the Mountain,* and *Mist of Mercy* prior to the accident, I would not have been prepared for the outcome. I am proud to say I am a lay apostle of Jesus Christ the Returning King! I believe I have been called to this mission. These messages are truly *Direction For Our Times.*

> *"My friends, Jesus allows struggle and difficulty in our lives and in our service to Him because He knows we can take it. He knows we won't quit. He can lean on us. Jesus needs to take His consolation where He can get it, so we must be at peace if He counts us as good friends who will accept a share of the cross with Him and continue to serve."*
> ~Mist of Mercy , page 41, Anne, a lay apostle

Suzanne S., AZ

Please join me in Prayer of Thanks to Our Lord, Jesus Christ! A true miracle has occurred!!

Last August (2008) my 18-year-old daughter, Mary and I did a little pilgrimage on our own to Holy Trinity Abbey. On our last night in Co. Cavan, we attended the lay apostles prayer group at St. Anne's in Bailieborough. After a beautiful hour of Adoration, Anne spoke. At the end of her talk, she added that we all needed to pray for marriages, especially the hard cases. She said if couples separate, they frustrate God's plan for their lives. Afterward my daughter and I both commented that as Anne spoke about this, she was looking directly at me.

You see, I came to Holy Trinity Abbey to beg Our Lord's direction - my husband and I have been married for 25 years, have 7 children and would definitely qualify as one of the "hard cases." My husband is from Tehran, Iran, is (was) Muslim and has either been indifferent or resistant to my faith (although he was fine about the children receiving all of their Sacraments). He is basically uninvolved in most areas of the kids' lives or our marriage. At some points in our marriage, he would join the children and me at Mass or at our nightly "family prayer." He has even been to Medjugorje twice! I went home from Ireland in tears, convinced that I was to remain in this marriage. I was given the grace to accept and totally trust even though it made no sense to me.

Last week, as my husband lay dying in a hospital with viral encephalitis, he asked to be baptized! Our Pastor baptized Ali and administered the Anointing of the Sick. Eight days later, Ali is now home. It is truly a miracle! Our children are beside themselves with joy and can't wait until their Dad can receive Our Lord in Holy Communion with them!

"My friends in the world know suffering. This will not change and it has always been this way. What separates My friends from those who walk without Me is the grace that accompanies My followers. If a soul is willing to accept heavenly grace, that soul's suffering is changed. Crosses carried in union with

heaven benefit both the individual soul and the world."
~Monthly Message, May 1, 2006, Jesus

Ray A.F.L.

If I had not been faithfully following our Lord's direction this past year, I don't believe I could have survived spiritually. Since last April I have lost my mother and both of my roommates to cancer. The past two Lenten seasons have been ones of living with Jesus' passion.

Mary Jo B., MN

The way the messages came to help me in my life was when both of my parents died this last year. I had just watched the *Mist of Mercy* when mom died. It gave me such peace. It really brought me to a place in my faith to accept death. I can actually celebrate my mom and dad's death knowing that even purgatory is a place of the Heavenly Kingdom and that souls are very happy to be there.

Helen F., UK

I was brought up a Catholic by two beautiful parents. I had a wonderful childhood, and as I grew my parents became my best friends. I always went to church, mainly because that's what we did. I went to college and while there started to doubt the authenticity of what I'd been taught regarding the Eucharist and that started me thinking much more about my religion. I still continued to go to Mass but stopped going to Communion. It seemed the best thing to do at the time because I couldn't accept what the Catholic Church taught. But I still wanted to be Catholic. I left college and continued going to church without receiving Holy Communion for years. Then my father became ill. He and my mother were the best testimonies for Christianity that I ever saw. My father was my rock. The thought of him not being around was always too much for me to think about so I blocked it out. His illness got worse over three years until he had to have a major operation to remove his spleen. He told me there was a 50% chance that he wouldn't come through the operation. He was 75 at the time and was trying to prepare me. The day of his operation I sat in our house with my mother, sister and brother waiting for the hospital to phone. It was one of the worst and best days of my life. He pulled through this major operation and within a couple of weeks was home with us. I came home from work one day to my brother who was very concerned about my father's elevated temperature. He wanted him to go to hospital to be checked. To cut a long story short, within 48 hours my father died of blood poisoning. To say I was devastated is an understatement. I honestly don't know how we survived his death. I became incredibly angry with God. He had put us through so much, allowed it to be ok and then took my father away just as we got him back. I stopped going to church and became incredibly bitter toward God.

About a year after my father died, my mother became ill. Slowly she got worse as the months went on and the doctors had no idea what was wrong with her. This beautiful, energetic and vibrant woman literally deteriorated in front of our eyes, and nobody could help us. One day a doctor discovered a lump in her stomach and she was diagnosed with pancreatic cancer. Because we loved her so much, the physical and mental suffering we experienced during the three years she was ill was unbelievable. As you can imagine, my bitterness toward God became even worse. Two of the most wonderful people in the world being treated so badly by someone they had always loved and followed. How could this be right? Then one day while my mother slept I began chatting with my aunt. She and my uncle had been going to Medjugorje for years and were full of their experiences. Up until this point I had no desire to even discuss such things but this particular day as I sat with my mother, my aunt began very gently to tell me about Medjugorje. When she finished, she went outside to make a cup of tea and I had this incredible urge to go to this place. This was a real turning point for me because I literally couldn't wait to get to church. I ran down the road to attend Mass. When I came back and told my mother I had been to church, the look on her face was one I'll never forget. She hadn't said a word to me about this in the three years I hadn't gone since my father's death. I feel I came back to the Church at a time to be helpful to my mother. My mother had always been an incredibly spiritual person and loved Our Lady so much but the suffering she had endured had taken its toll on her. I remember sitting on her bed reading testimonies about Medjugorje to her. I couldn't get enough of this and she relished them too. Unfortunately my beautiful mother died in July 2001. Her death left me once more devastated. However, this time I didn't feel the need to turn away from God. I turned to him. I had a thirst for reading spiritual books that still continues and it was through this thirst that I heard about Anne a lay apostle and *Direction For Our Times*. I have read all her books, and I literally cried when I read about her journeys to Heaven with Jesus.

I receive the Holy Eucharist in a completely different way than I used to, and I go to Confession once a month. I recently asked in my prayers for help in my prayer life and especially the Rosary. I wanted to say the Rosary each day, but somehow it never seemed to happen. Then out of the blue came reasons for me to say the rosary every day (one concerning the Abortion Bill being discussed in the USA) and as devotion for the sick. I now understand that good people do suffer and that this isn't necessarily a bad thing - it unites them to Jesus and His sufferings. My only regret is that I didn't understand this at the time of my parents' sufferings because I would have offered it all on their behalf to God.

My uncle recently died, but while we were sitting with him in the hospital I took hold of his hand and in my head I offered his sufferings to Our Lord. I know this will have helped him to get to Heaven. I am now a content, peaceful person.

In each life there comes difficult moments and sorrowful situations. I am there, steadying you. I provide great graces when great graces are needed."

~Serving in Clarity, September 13, 2006, pg. 25, Jesus

Janet C., CA

I am raising my two teenage grandsons and try to read pages from the *Volumes* to them often. But my testimony is about their mother. My oldest daughter, Debbie is 39 and has led a troubled adult life. She is currently in jail in Phoenix, AZ, and will be there for months. About six months ago, I had the *DFOT* office send her several *Volumes*. The result has been amazing! The area where she is housed is a "block." The women are in their cells 23 hours a day (some by choice, some not) and only leave the cell once a day for an hour. Debbie started with *Climbing the Mountain* and then the *Volumes* and has really found "salvation" in Our Lord's messages. She has shared this with the other women in the "block" (6 to 9 women, some of whom come and go) and the result has been unbelievable. The women pray (through vents in the walls), share scripture verses, the thoughts from *DFOT*, and have formed a choir, which has a repertoire of almost a dozen hymns. Debbie tells me the guards are amazed at the change that has taken place in C - block. When new women come in "cussing and swearing," the women talk to them about Jesus, pray with them and, apparently, each one has come to the Lord in her own way. I can hardly believe some of the stories these women have to tell and how a prison group of lay apostles have helped them. I am so eternally grateful to God for giving Anne and all of us *DFOT* and I know there in the Arizona women's prison, it is saving souls.

I wish to talk to those imprisoned, for any reason. Dear brothers and sisters, your Christian family needs you. Your prayers,

your sacrifices have great power. If you unite your suffering to Me, I can use it to save many souls.
~Heaven Speaks To Prisoners, July 25, 2005, Jesus

Jodi G., MN

I have shared the *Volumes* and other books with many friends and family.

My husband, our two adult children and I pray the Morning Offering, as well as the Allegiance Prayer. It puts us in contact with God from the moment we awake in the morning. We started out with the prayers taped to our bathroom mirror, but now they are written on our hearts, and when my morning alarm goes off, it is the first thing I pray/say before I get out of bed.

My daughter's best friend Amy had become an agnostic after David a good friend of theirs was killed at age 17 in a car accident four years ago. We began to pray the lay apostle prayers for her and after nearly a year of praying, we decided it was time to give her the *Volumes*, *Climbing the Mountain* and *Mist of Mercy*. She called us the first week crying and thanking us for saving her life and soul and how eternally grateful she was. She continues on her journey with God and has drawn her whole family closer to Him. Her husband now goes to church with her and is on his way to being a baptized and confirmed Catholic.

My friend, there are events in every life that stand out as difficult and life-altering. This tragedy, this abrupt change of course, will stand out to you, I know. When you feel a sense of shock, a sense of stunning upset in your life, you must look for Me. I am there.
~ Heaven Speaks to Those Who Suffer Tragedy,
December 12, 2006 Jesus

Maria P., NY

I was born in Warsaw, Poland. When I was 17 years old I gave birth to my son, Dominik and became a single parent. I came to the US when I was almost 21 years old with my son and made our home here. I was raising and supporting Dominik by myself for 13 years. We struggled often from financial needs and emotionally as well. I always tried to keep "things" together by working extra hours. I often worried about Dominik staying home alone. My faith in God at that time kept us going. I prayed and hoped that things would get better. We attended Mass on Sundays and Holy Days. God answered my prayers when I met my loving husband, Greg. When Dominik was 13 years old, I gave birth to our son, Anthony. Somehow we became lukewarm Catholics not always attending Mass on Sundays and growing apart from our church. When Anthony went to kindergarten I got a job as a Real Estate Professional to help us financially. I was working many hours, and I was growing apart from my family.

The wakeup call came on December 13, 2005, when on one cold night Dominik left home and never came back. Police knocked on our door at four in the morning and we had to drive to the police precinct to find out that our son, Dominik died in automobile accident. Shock, denial, disbelief, anger and grief were left for me. I had to learn how to deal with it. I didn't know how to go on but yet I knew that I must go on for Anthony and for my husband. I resented God. I was so angry I called Our Lord a monster at one time and even denied His existence. I didn't want to go church any longer but did it just because Anthony was preparing for his First Communion.

Thank God that my husband took over, for without Greg, Anthony wouldn't have made his First Communion that year. I wasn't capable of preparing him.

In the summer 2006 my parents came for a visit from Poland and to help me. I was a wreck, emotionally and physically.

Thank God for my mom. She has a real gift of faith. One day when we were at the cemetery by Dominik's grave, my mom was praying and I was angry with her for doing so. I couldn't pray. I wanted her to stop praying and stop crying. My mom told me her faith is her treasure. My reply to her was that I wished to have faith like her too, so I could be with my son again just for that reason alone. Somehow the seed was planted in me and my search for God had begun.

On October 2006 my husband's cousin, Michele gave us a DVD of Anne, a lay apostle on Tele Care. When I heard her speaking something melted in my heart, and I asked my husband to find out about the *Volumes,* which he did and ordered for me. When the *Volumes* arrived and I started to read, I knew that God granted me my wish. He was talking to me and I couldn't stop reading and sharing with my husband and Anthony as well. Things in my small family started to change; we started to pray in the mornings and read Anne's *Volumes* along with the Bible.

My complete conversion happened when I read *Volume Four: "Jesus Speaks to Sinners,"* and I went to Confession. After Volume Six I quit my job to be a wife to my husband and a mother to Anthony. I also felt in my heart that Our Lord personally called me to become a Eucharistic Minister when I was praying before the Blessed Sacrament, which I became later. It was just the beginning. All three of us became "lay apostles of Jesus Christ returning King." We pray the rosary each evening, read the message from Our Lord together each month and go to Confession monthly. I try to do my Adoration before the Blessed Sacrament once a week. My husband works to support our small family, and we still share what we can with others.

God is so good to us and blesses us each day. I am forever grateful to Our Lady. I know she helped me to find Jesus. I'm forever grateful to Our Lord Jesus, for saving me. I'm also grateful for my mom who never stopped praying for me and for my husband who never gave up on me and always gives me support. I'm still grieving as it has only been three years since Dominik went with Our Lord. But going to Mass each morning to receive Our Lord in Communion gives me strength and healing to go on and help others as well. Certainly I would be lost without God and without His healing power. My life would make no sense whatsoever. In conclusion of my testimony I will say what one of our priests at St. Rose of Lima said in one of his homilies: "THANK GOD FOR GOD."

(Note: Maria has dedicated a website to her son Dominik. See the Appendix for more information.)

Pam B., CA

I had the great honor and privilege of receiving the set of *Volumes* late last summer. I cannot tell you how they have affected my spiritual life. It was as though Heaven opened up and God the Father, Jesus, Blessed Mother and various saints were reaching down delivering these incredible messages. I love to read them while I am at Eucharistic Adoration. With the way things are going in this turbulent world, I find so much comfort in the pages of these books. After I finished reading all of the *Volumes*, I started over again. I've had many challenges and crosses with family and personal tragedies. I have been suffering with acute Fibromyalgia for 18 years now and my body is so tired from carrying this pain. But I use the pain as prayer for many intentions. In addition to the *Volumes*, I am reading Anne's books, *The Mist of Mercy* and *Climbing the Mountain*. These books have also given me comfort and hope.

> *"Dearest little apostles, be at peace in your weariness. Heaven understands that you sometimes feel tired. When you feel tired, you must understand that heaven is not tired. When you feel discouraged, you must under-*

161

stand that heaven is not tired...Be at peace in this."

~Serving in Clarity, page 31, *Blessed Mother,* October 27, 2006

Yolanda B., TX

I keep my copy of *Volume One* with me at all times (in my car and at home). I try to read something from *DFOT* every day, as it is part of my prayer life. When I miss a few days, I notice something is missing, and I pick up one of the *Volumes* and read. Anytime there's a crisis situation, I ask God to show me what I need to read at that time. I then open Volume One knowing the book will open onto the appropriate page. It always does. The messages I read address exactly whatever internal suffering or confusion, and as to why, I am instantly changed. My perspective changes and I feel such a peaceful, loving presence. I then feel grateful for the situation and elated with love for Jesus, for the Blessed Virgin and confident that God has a purpose for this situation.

There are so many powerful instances of this nature, but I'll only share one right now. Five days ago my mother, 84 years young, suffered a massive heart attack. She had triple bypass surgery to stop blood in her lungs; her kidneys failed, and she's been on a respirator. My parents are raising my 11-year-old nephew – they've raised him since he was 3 days old. The concern for my father and nephew as well was traumatic. A couple of days later I had a horrible pain on the top of my head, was exhausted, had difficulty breathing, and could not bear what they were going through, as well as the fear for my nephew's situation.

I picked up my *Volume One* and opened a page, knowing I'd receive instant help. As always, I did. The book opened to page 113, to the following highlighted section: "You must not worry about your health. I can bestow good health upon you if I wish you to have it. There are times when it is more important for the coming of My Kingdom that you suffer."

My head pain immediately stopped completely for a couple of hours. When it returned I was OK with it – it lasted about 6 more hours. But, receiving that message transformed all my other pain in an instant. I'm not saying I'm thrilled with what my mother and family are going through, but my perspective changed and everything was tolerable.

> *Pain is a universal experience. Hurt is a universal experience. You are not alone in your pain and in your hurt.*
> ~Heaven Speaks About Addictions, page 7, St. Barnabas

G.A., East Coast

In the October 2006 monthly message, Jesus says, 'I am with you.' It's the same as the Sacred Heart mission, echoed. 'Your God, your Creator, speaks this message in so many ways. In everyday grace you must hear My voice saying I am with you.' I pray every night before I go to bed, 'help me listen so I can wake up in the morning to hear you say, I am with you.' This is an exercise I am trying to put into practice. This has helped me with so many crosses and hardships. Especially in regard to my daughter who is a recovering addict. For almost a year now, the Lord is consuming her more and more. Anyway, she went to jail. When they clicked the handcuffs on her, it was just like being at the crucifixion and Mary standing there watching. They pulled my daughter's little arms behind her back (she is very tiny – those who are on crack and other hard drugs, are nothing but skin and bones). Click, click. I could hear the handcuffs. I thought I died. I wondered why no one had thrown dirt in my face yet. But, immediately I thought about the Blessed Mother watching the same thing. That is what saved me, Mary. Then they dragged my daughter away. She was looking over her shoulder and was so pathetic. I thought I died. I don't know how I was putting one foot in front of the other. My husband and I were in silence. When we moved, he suggested getting a hamburger. I remember thinking, "why does he want to eat?" We went, but I don't remember eating anything. The next morning, I was standing in the kitchen and could see the picture of the Sacred Heart. I have never raised my voice to Him, but I said, 'Jesus, what was wrong with us? We just sat there in all this pain (by the picture of the Sacred Heart the day before). Why didn't we renew our consecration to you? Why didn't we fall on our knees and ask you for mercy? Why didn't we pray to Your Sacred Heart? All we did was sit there in pain.' And then I had this image in my mind. I saw myself on the couch and I saw Him sitting right next to me with His arm around me. He turned to me and said, " I knew. I was with you." I know those words were real. That was a total gift. I saw Him sitting with me. I called my spiritual director and told him. He said, 'what did His voice sound like?' Never had anyone asked me the tone of Jesus' voice. I said, I have never heard a voice with such compassion. From that moment on, I became very aware of His tone. You can't have compassion if you don't have love. So, the words, "I am with you" are real. This and the Morning Offering have sustained me every day. This apostolate has changed me.

Ann M., KY

I have long been faithful to serving the Church and after becoming aware of Jesus the Returning King messages, I have been a devoted promoter of the mission by spreading the volumes. A couple of weeks before Christmas my 44-year old son died in a house fire. He also was a well-loved member of our small town Catholic community. I was particularly close to this son, sharing many things spiritually with the same heart.

Six weeks after the loss of my son John, I unexpectedly lost my daughter, Trish.

In dealing with this extreme grief, the thing that helped me the most, actually held me together, were the messages and *Mist of Mercy*. I received the grace to choose hope rather then despair, to choose strength rather than pity. I took this opportunity to witness to others, heaven. Not only as our goal, but also the friendship we have with the saints there to guide us along and uphold us. I became more and more aware of my ability to choose how I feel and chose to look to heaven and feel the hope we are called to.

I only have humble gratitude for the graces received from this mission. As I am working though this profound grief, I read the messages daily in order to stay strengthened in the consolation that both my children are together again, working for the Kingdom of God, just as they did on earth.

Note: Ann's son John T. Mudd wrote a book of prayers before he passed away. She sent me one and it is quite beautiful and filled with his love for Christ. For information on how to get a copy of the small bound book, please see link in the Appendix. ~Bonnie

Depression

Remember that if a soul is not united to Me, that soul feels a gaping emptiness, a loneliness, and a sadness.
~Volume Two, August 29, 2003, Jesus

My children in the world can become discouraged and sad. Dearest little ones, if you are this way, you must come to Me and rest your worries in My heart. I do not like to see you sad, even though life can be difficult.
~Heaven Speaks About Depression,
August 8, 2005, Jesus

Carmel R., England

A series of events brought me to this Mission. It was then I realized that heaven had been at work!

Some years ago my house in the Aire Valley in the north of England was flooded. At midnight, as October became November, the river raged through our row of houses and was terrifying. I was away from home for 6½ months with my beloved pets in kennels while the property was dried out and renovated. Having a history of clinical depression, this trauma took its toll on my health and the sight of the river rising whenever it rained terrified me. The house was also too big for me, my son having left home. Due to this, I unfortunately had to retire early through ill-health. I had been away from the Church for a number of years, and was trying to find my way back. However, I had no car, and as I was living in a small village in the Pennine hills, public transport wasn't good. However, I carried on as best I could. Eventually, I decided to move. This became complicated, and it was near desperation, which brought me to look in Huddersfield, a town I knew nothing about. After moving in, I was amazed to discover that the Catholic Church was less than a five minute walk from my house. Looking at a local map, I noticed a Convent a few streets away. I was astonished to learn that it was a Presentation Convent; my late Aunt had been a Presentation Sister! At this point my life changed completely. I was drawn in to the Church and the Convent, which I now refer to as my second home. The welcome from the Sisters and parishioners has been overwhelming. This is where I met Sr. Elizabeth Tuttle who has done so much for the lay apostolate in England. Sr. Elizabeth found numerous other Sisters who had known my Aunt, even though she had spent nearly all of the 60 years of her religious life in Pakistan, and had died about 16 years earlier! One of these is the Sister who took the Volumes to Pope John Paul II! When Sr. Elizabeth told me about "Anne" and the *Volumes*, I believed it immediately because it came from her. Since then, I have tried to live my life as asked by heaven through the Volumes and monthly messages from Jesus, and I attempt to do anything that is asked of me for the Mission. I have been privileged to drive Sr. Elizabeth at times to her talks, thus learning much about it. This was useful too as on one occasion, when Sr. Elizabeth was unwell, I was able to give one of the talks in her absence. This Mission has brought me closer to the Lord than I ever thought possible. I have to admit, I'm not keen on the area I live in, as it's more built up than I'm used to, although my life is happy and fulfilled, and I should be content with that. However, I started to look at property in other places within reach of this, until one day I was reading a message from God the Father in *Volume Four* and came to the following:

"Never wish yourself somewhere else as I have chosen

the exact place to use you in My Kingdom. " Message received and understood!

> *When you see Christians who claim to be following Me, but they are sad and morose, you should be alert. Despair and depression do not come from Me. My followers are given hope and a lightness of spirit, despite difficulties. If you, yourself, notice you are feeling sad more often, it is because you are not connected to Me through prayer and the sacraments.*
> ~Volume One, page 87, Jesus

Francie C.

Late last summer I was being attacked by the demonic to a terrible state of depression and hurt. I had allowed myself to become vulnerable to a situation when I preferred to remain neutral. Being only human I needed super spiritual powers to help me out of this state of hell on earth into which I had fallen.

It was so awful I couldn't stand myself or my grief. My soul couldn't stand being in this state any longer. I kept praying to feel His joy again, to help me get rid of this controlling spirit that had attached itself to the depths of my heart. Once I reached my work place, I reached for my headphones and immediately went to the website for *Direction for Our Times.* There I found my Jesus alive and able to speak to me.

These were beautiful words of Jesus given to Anne a lay apostle. I listened to them over and over again. It was as though the voice of the priest reading the message had been overshadowed by the spirit of Our Lord, Jesus Christ. Through his voice I heard my Lord speaking to me. I am thankful for the ability to hear and for the obedience of Anne to publish His word so all who wish can hear His word. The September 1, 2008, message was the one I needed to hear.

I let my heart fall on each word until I could feel His Joy again. One thing I understand is that the Lord allows us to feel His pain, sorrow and hurt. And, when we feel it is too much to bear. All we have to do is to ask for His Joy to come back. What a blessing to be in the pits and then pulled out so quickly! Thank you Lord for your words and encouragement.

> *My children in the world can become discouraged and sad. Dearest little ones, if you are this way, you must come to Me and rest your worries in My heart. I do not like to see you sad, even though life can be difficult. You feel you are alone and that is part of the reason why you feel such sadness. But you are never alone because I never leave you.*
> ~Heaven Speaks About Depression,
> August 8, 2005 Jesus

Heidi

I attended a day of Eucharistic Renewal with Anne on Saturday, January 14, 2006. I don't remember exactly where it was held, but I think that it was in St. Veronica's Church in South San Francisco, California. As usual when attending any religious conferences, I was alone. It was a rainy, gray day, which seemed to accentuate being alone.

My work/career involves counseling individuals, couples, families and adolescents around issues such as depression, anxiety, communication problems, behavior problems and helping to develop skills needed to resolve or lessen the problem. It can be quite challenging at times. I work for a non-profit agency so I am able to offer my services for a very low price to those who would not be able to afford a therapist otherwise.

So, I was very interested in hearing Anne speak. An added pleasure was hearing, for the first time, the beautiful voice of Mark Forrest. As Mr. Forrest sang, "You Are Mine," I closed my eyes and looked down, listening carefully to the words. They really touched me and as I listened, I began to feel very much alone, even though the room was full. I felt cold and noticed that my shoulders were beginning to hunch over and I felt heaviness on my back. About that time, I "saw" me hunched over and saw all my clients pile onto my back. Then I saw all my family. I particularly remember my children, mother and husband, piling on my back, too. Just when I was thinking, "no wonder it feels so heavy," I saw Jesus come down and in one swoop, take all who were on my back and put them on His back. In a second, I knew the Truth -- I was never alone and it was Jesus doing the work. He, after all, could not hand off all the people to anyone else. He carried them all the time. I just carried them temporarily. I "awoke" from this experience with tears streaming down my face and gratefulness in my heart for His love and compassion for me. The words to "You Are Mine" felt so personal, as if God really spoke to me and reached my soul through them. When I came back from the conference, I told my husband of my vision. He scoffed when I told him about my family being piled on my shoulders. Little did I know I was to experience the most difficult year of my life in 2006 when in October, my beloved daughter told my husband and me that she is bisexual and was involved with a girl. My son later told us that he is gay and has a same sex partner, as well. These were devastating blows to us. After my daughter's revelation, my husband began coming to Mass with me every Sunday and also observes Holy Days of Obligation and Feast days. We don't know where this journey will take us, but it has brought him and me closer together. My mother has also been a great source of support as well as a few friends. However, the only thing that really sustains me is the vision of Jesus taking them and placing them on His shoulders.

You did not become sad like this in a moment. Come to Me all throughout your day

and allow Me to help you carry this heavy cross of sadness.
~Heaven Speaks About Depression, August 8, 2005, Jesus

Victoria L., MD

I suffer from depression and loneliness. At times I even feel suicidal. I long for Heaven. But the Lord must have work for me to do so He will take me when he wants.

Sometimes I feel I must be doing something right if the devil wants to kill me off so much! But the Lord protects me. I find the writings very helpful in the areas of depression and the temptation of suicidal thoughts. St. Margaret Mary Alacoque and others have also been helpful in this area when I pray to them. I pray I will have the grace to stay on this path and keep climbing the mountain.

Only I, the Divine Healer can heal you. I can give you nourishment that will set your soul alight again. Come to Me in all trust.
~Heaven Speaks About Depression
August 8, 2005, Jesus

Anxiety

Fear, anxiety, restlessness do not come from Me.
~Volume Two, August 28, 2003, Jesus

Jesus is concerned about the fastness of today's world. It provides distraction and causes the spirit to move constantly, never pausing and recollecting itself. This is why so many of our children struggle with anxiety. Remember that anxiety never comes from God and is a sure sign that something is amiss in the way you are living.
~Volume One, page 98, Blessed Mother

Edward, Philippines

I don't really remember how I came across the messages from Anne. But, one thing is for sure - while reading the messages I felt something stir which I have never felt before. It's as if you could hear a voice while reading the messages. The free e-books (*Volumes and Heaven speaks to...*) really helped me when I was down. I am currently recovering from anxiety disorder and reading the messages gave me peace of mind and concrete guidance how to live my faith in this dark time.

Before I had the anxiety disorder, I was a man of the world; prideful and arrogant. I didn't respect my parents and engaged in fornication. I only cared about myself and was indifferent to the plight of people with problems. I was a "nominal" Catholic so to speak, going to Mass because it was an obligation and because I feared going to hell. Then when I had severe panic attacks I wasn't able to function normally. It was a wake up call to change my life. Jesus' messages from Anne played a large role in my mental and spiritual recovery. It brought comfort as well as encouragement at a time I needed it most.

As of now, because of God's Grace, I have made peace with my parents and strive to honor them as best as I can. It became my mission to live the Gospel. And I'm now in a Pre-Catechumenate program under the Catholic Church through the Neo-Catechumenal Way to learn more about our Catholic Faith and to live it fully.

I want you to say "no" to anxiety and distress. My children can rest peacefully in my arms these days, as Jesus fulfills His plan for the salvation of the world.

~Volume One, July 2, 2003, Blessed Mother

Gina P.

I have been quite ill for many years. I suffer each and every day and often my problems are totally debilitating. Before reading the *Volumes,* and becoming a Catholic, I could not cope at all. Now, I still have my bad days, but the majority of the time I cope amazingly. Also, I used to let insensitive people and people who would constantly get angry with me for petty reasons, bother me a great deal. I would expend too much energy trying to make them see how they hurt me and why. I'm totally over that now. It doesn't matter to me anymore if people like me or if they sympathize with how difficult my life is. For the first time I feel completely united to Christ and secure in the love He has for me. And I now love and accept myself, so I no longer need confirmation from others to feel good about myself. I can't tell you the freedom this has given me. I will read and reread the *Volumes* all my life just as I do the Bible. Only God's words can transform a person like this. To Him be all the Glory.

Denial

Take my hand, little child of my heart, and your mother will lead you to every spiritual success. Truly, you will not even believe how we intend to change your life.
~Volume One, July 15, 2003 Blessed Mother

I am Jesus. I am God. I am complete in Myself. I am present in your world and I am present in heaven. You see, I am omnipresent. Even if you wish to, you cannot remove yourself from My presence on earth.
~Heaven Speaks to Those Who Don't Know
December 21, 2006, Jesus

Donna B. LA

I had picked up *Climbing The Mountain (CTM)*. I saw the book, but had always been suspect of locutions, apparitions and miracles. I never liked the tone of them. In all the years I worked as manager in the bookstore, so many people would come in and dwell on the mysteries, miracles and apparitions. No one ever talked about Jesus. It was a big turnoff for me. I tended to dump it in the spiritual wasteland of good, but not necessarily good for me. I never saw it as a vehicle of grace. So, I saw the collection of *Volumes* and books, opened *CTM,* read a few pages and thinking that it was nice, put it back. The first thing I looked for was the Imprimatur. I didn't see the Imprimatur on the copyright page, but flipped the next page and there was the "disclaimer" about Anne being obedient to the bishop, the Holy Father, the Magisterium of the Church. I thought that was good. It was encouraging that Anne was obedient. I put the book back and went to Adoration. (When you come back to the Lord, the work is tremendous and you grow. You've been like a dried up seed in the ground and then the rains come and you become a weed in the garden. I began to see His hand in everything. The veil fell off once again as always happens.) I walked into the Adoration Chapel, said hello to Jesus, turned around and to my right and there on the shelf was everything Anne wrote. There was a huge sign posted that said "Please do not leave books in the chapel. All books on this bookshelf have to be approved by Father Bill." All the books, *Volumes*, and even the *Heaven Speaks* series were there. Not only are they there, but, they are all worn out, frayed. They have been so used that the pages were falling out. They all had a big sticker on the front saying, "Do not remove from Adoration chapel." So, the next day I couldn't wait for the bookstore to open. I peered in the window and saw all of Anne's *Volumes*. But the store wasn't open that day. I went home and couldn't sleep. The next day I went and bought sixty dollars worth of books. That night I wrote in my journal after starting to read *CTM*. This is the scenario: 11:00 pm, I was reading where Jesus took Anne to heaven – when I finished the last description of heaven, I began to cry. I was so overcome with joy I couldn't believe it. At that moment, I received the gifts of faith, hope and love. I, absolutely, 100%, for the first time, KNEW what Jesus had been saying, that God is real. It wasn't always a certainty for me. The feeling was overwhelming. If I had to add up all the hours I spent pursuing this, I'm sure it would be in the hundreds of thousands. I have devoted my life to the pursuit of God's Truth. I went and locked myself in the bathroom and just cried. I'm bipolar, and I didn't want my husband to think I was having an episode. This is what I wrote at 11:00 pm, Friday, Feb. 13th: I must document, on this very day, how a few hours ago, Jesus with all of heaven witnessing, bestowed upon me – body, soul, heart and mind –

the graces of true faith, hope and charity. I felt as if God had completely consumed me in the fire of His love with an inextinguishable fire.

All of your faith, all of your sacrifices, and all of your
dutiful acts are justified and rewarded.
~Volume Seven, July 10, 2004, St. Anthony

Kathy G., CA

It was a depressing New Year, January of 2007. I had just found out I was pregnant with our fourth child, my husband was self-employed and our Cobra insurance would run out a few months before the baby would be born. Where would we get the estimated $10,000 to pay for the birth of the baby? We were living paycheck to paycheck. Somehow, I found myself on an airplane to Malibu, California for a retreat with "Anne," a lay apostle. My brother offered to pay for my plane ticket. On the airplane I prayed. I told God I didn't know anything about this woman, "Anne." Even though I was impressed with her first Volume, I was nervous about whether or not she was a fake. I told God I was in a bad state of affairs. Not only was I pregnant, hormonal and short on money, but angry at my mother for not calling me over the past year after I told her I was going to work on my childhood sexual abuse issues. As soon as I found out I was pregnant, I began an intense 12 Step Study so I could get through the Steps of AA completely before the baby came. The abuse issues were coming up, and I was going to have to deal with them with or without my mother. It was as if she had abandoned me when I needed her most. I hadn't done a lot of work on this particular issue, but God had been preparing me by bringing things to the surface over a period of time. I was overwhelmed because I felt I couldn't take care of the three children I already had.

I am a recovering alcoholic and had sobered up ten days before my oldest son's first birthday. It had been difficult to get to meetings over the years with the children being so young and almost two years apart. I had seven and a half years sobriety and was looking forward to all the children going to school full time the following year. I would be able to go to as many AA meetings, counseling, church groups, etc. as I needed to. I was a wreck. I needed time to work on my spiritual life, and now it was being ripped away from me with this latest pregnancy. "God, why now?" My husband and I had been avoiding pregnancy using Natural Family Planning and trusting in the Lord that He knew what was best for us. I began to have doubts.

I arrived in Malibu and the talks began. I was impressed with the idea of this Rescue Mission. Anne spoke very well as did Fr. Darragh. During a break in the afternoon, I began to walk through the "Way of the Cross" garden. I wasn't praying the Stations of the Cross but just looking at the large, marble statues of each station. I came to the fourth station where Jesus meets His mother, and I broke down and began to cry. I realized that Mary could not take away her Son's pain no matter how badly she wanted to. My mother, in woundedness from her own childhood, could not be there to help ease my pain. But I had a Heavenly Mother, Mary, who could help me walk through this pain. Even though I was a cradle Catholic, I had never had a devotion to Mary or a relationship with her. Jesus gave me His Mother there in the garden that afternoon. Later that evening, after Benediction, "Anne" and Fr. Darragh were praying over people in front of the Eucharist. I decided I better go up since I had a pretty emotional afternoon. As they began to pray, once again I began to cry. I suddenly had the desire to pray the rosary! What a shocker! Where did that come from? I had beaten myself up for years over the fact that I hated the rosary. I was repulsed by it. Growing up, we said the rosary every night. We had to kneel for the whole 20 minutes and if we got tired and sat back on our feet for a moment, we were yelled at by my father's booming military voice, "Kneel up!" I hated every minute of it and it was even worse when I was told to "offer it up." Once I left home, "never again," I thought, "will I say the rosary." I had never stopped going to Mass, but my faith was severely lacking. I had no expectations when I went on the retreat because I didn't know what I needed. But God did. He gave me His Mother, the power of the rosary and healed a wound from my childhood. It put me on the road to forgiving my mother and having compassion for her. It seems so long ago, now, that I was introduced to Anne, and the rescue mission. So many blessings have come since that first healing. The *Volumes* and monthly messages have given me clear direction on how to open myself up to God's will. As a lay apostle, the Lord is now preparing me to be His vessel in carrying the message of love and mercy to others.

PART THREE

Healing of Relationships

Forgiving Others
Receiving Forgiveness

Forgiving Others

It is clear to Me that many suffer from hidden wounds. The only way for these wounds to heal is for the carrier of the wound to forgive the one who inflicted the injury.
~Heaven Speaks to Those Who Struggle To Forgive,
December 13, 2006, Jesus

I can help poor sinners to forgive them-selves and seek the forgiveness of my Son, a forgiveness that heals and strengthens.
~Volume One, page 92, Blessed Mother

Judy M., FL

I struggled for 20 years with my sister-in-law. We had a pretty toxic relationship. Every time we saw each other, which occurred often because we're an Italian family and live close to each other, she threw some kind of hurt my way. As much as I was willing to forgive, I always held on to the pain a little. After many years of forgiving, sometimes I felt I couldn't do it anymore. My husband and I had a big argument one night about it, and he wasn't understanding of my hurt. I tried at length to explain it was putting a wedge between us in our relationship. It wasn't right. I was his wife and he should understand what I was going through, but he couldn't. So we struggled to the point that sometimes I didn't go to family gatherings. I needed to stay away from the hurt so it wouldn't get worse. Then, last year my sister-in-law was diagnosed with cancer. Through the grace of God, I knew that I totally, without question, needed to give my anger with her to the Lord. He forgave us by dying for the sins we were going to commit. I remember reading about a saint that said 'we only love Jesus as much as the person we love the least in our lives.' That struck me. I had to say it at least ten times in my head. I said this at our lay apostle group and it actually helped other people with their struggles as it makes us see things differently. I had to willingly and lovingly serve her by helping her with her illness and spending time with her every day, so she wouldn't be alone. I took the day shift. The first time I went, there was a part of me, as much as I wanted to do it, I didn't want to do it. That first day we shared and we talked. I just tried to love her.

As I was leaving, she kissed me and thanked me. She really meant it. Then she told me she loved me and I couldn't say it back because I wasn't ready. I was really shocked. I knew I loved her but not the way Jesus wanted me to. I had to pray on that and remembered that love and forgiveness are an actions required of us. I wanted to do it willingly. When I went back the second day, I still couldn't say it. But, by the third day, I could. Even though I went through all the actions of taking care of her and helping her, I started to look forward to it. We said our sorry's, and I let everything go. I gave all the lingering resentment to God. It changed everything. I realized that love is an action. Love is a choice. It was a time I felt the closest to Jesus, feeling what he probably went through, how He was treated and how He treated others. I felt so Christ like. I know I could have never ever done that before the *Volumes*. It would have been impossible. I'm a sinner. It just shows I am human and didn't have the grace to forgive her. He gave me the grace. It was so freeing. I was so excited to be able to do it for Him. Since then, I always say I have no problems because I give them to God. I just serve Him however He wants me to. It could have been me in that bed. What would I have done? I knew in her heart it was hard because it was for me. She had to accept me helping and taking care of her. And it was a big deal. I'll never forget that love is a choice. *Volume Seven* is my personal favorite without a doubt. It's because we can't do it alone. We know we have all the help of heaven, and all the help of the angels. I know they are all rooting for us all the time. It is true. And now my sister-in-law is one of those saints in heaven I hope, by now.

> *I want to explain something to you so that you know that we understand your predicament. Your difficulty in forgiving is understandable. I had to forgive those who crucified my Son.*
> ~Heaven Speaks To Those Who Struggle To Forgive,
> page 13, Blessed Mother

Karen, FL

Sometime in 2006, I became acquainted with *Volume One: Thoughts on Spirituality*, from *Direction for Our Times*. Within ten minutes the Lord had my undivided attention and was locked in my soul. It took only the gentle words of truth to clarify for me the undeniable message from our Shepherd. He beckons all of us to listen and take into our hearts the beautiful call on our lives as lay apostles that is given to us at Baptism.

I found more grace with reading each volume and a yearning to become more of what Jesus was asking. The astonishing quality that Jesus is speaking directly and exclusively to my soul was a gift I could not deny, and a much welcomed comfort.

I wondered if I could tackle deeper problems -- Bereft with certain crosses in our family of chronic illness, loss of work, and the alienation of a family member that embraced loose living was debilitating for my soul. Trusting Jesus through the storms of life is a great spiritual challenge for me and possibly a sin of weak faith. With each reading and prayer I found a steady gain of acknowledgment that I was being heard by my

Lord. In addition, I discovered a new desire and willingness to ask for the strength to change in the *way Jesus needed me to*. How amazed I was when, through His grace, I perceived changes in the way I approached the one who had trampled and betrayed my heart. I wanted to return kindness, gentleness and love, instead of stern warnings and criticism against serious lifestyle behavior. I could not have imagined, nor relished, forgiveness as a tender mercy became joyful and freeing for me to bestow. Jesus regularly works miracles of spiritual richness in our lives. Often, before I can even think of the words, my heart opens with gratitude for the lovely treasures Jesus generously gives in more abundance than I can fathom. It becomes particularly apparent during the times I can be with Jesus totally during adoration. It is not a feeling, but a silent presence of awe that I behold Him in the tabernacle. Admittedly, bringing my weariness and sufferings to our Lord continues regularly, but I have contentment knowing that this 'substance' unites me to Him. Jesus clearly showed me that His calm and gentle ways are best and I could always count on it, even when in personal turmoil.

The insightful revelations continue as I now see the seamless nature of how the saints in heaven are part of our armament to call upon and intercede for our needs. Jesus' compassionate heart for us, His children, is unfailing on earth and an eternal promise for our future in Heaven.

What does forgiveness bring? I will tell you. Forgiveness brings peace. Forgiveness brings self-acceptance because you are able to say, "Yes, this bad thing happened to me. Yes, it was hurtful and I suffered pain because of it." Then you stop and say, "No. I will not allow this injury to suffocate the goodness in me. No. I will not allow it to divert me from God's will in my life.

~Heaven Speaks To Those Who Struggle To Forgive,
page 7, St. Faustina

184

T. M., UK

I was at a charismatic conference and I saw the books by Anne, a lay apostle. They were going quickly and I wondered what they were about. I asked the man who ran the store what they were. He said a housewife in America started a lay apostolate. To make a long story short, I read the books. The one that affected me the most is, *Mist of Mercy*. I have a ministry focused on healing the family tree and the souls in purgatory. I pray a lot for the souls in purgatory. I pray with people because there is generational bondage. I had a terrible childhood myself. I've had to do a lot of forgiving. My husband was a surgeon and it has been a lonely and difficult marriage. About 15 years ago he had an affair with a girl my daughter's age. I thought I was going to die. The pain was so terrible. I've had lots of prayer for healing of my childhood, his affair, etc, but still had difficulty forgiving. Last year I chose a day to focus on forgiveness. I asked the Lord to please help me to really forgive. I picked up the blue *Volume*, and saw a message to those who had been abused. And do you know, I was able to forgive. It was amazing. I've always wanted to forgive. I have felt solidarity with this movement. I feel the closeness of Jesus. I've been spiritually alone for so long. I've been married for 45 years and run a very busy household. It's very hard work. Sometimes I get tired of it. Suddenly there is lightness in my touch. I can serve with such joy. This apostolate has completely changed my life.

Juli H.

I have been able to forgive my spouse (I am no longer married) and other people who betrayed me, and include them in my daily prayers for redemption.

You see, my friend, the path of bitterness leads in the opposite direction of where you must go. Come our way, to heaven, and you will have joy. The enemy seeks

185

to divert you by encouraging you to persist in bitter self-righteousness and indignation. You know that it is not Jesus who advises you to hold on to anger. It is His enemy, who is also your enemy.
~Heaven Speaks To Those Who Struggle To Forgive, page 8, St. Faustina

Keri B.

I have forgiven myself.

Bonnie, NJ

Through reading *Climbing the Mountain*, pp. 70-71, I have found the blueprint for forgiving a very difficult person (my father's wife) who has hurt me, and with whom I have been angry. So often we are told that we must forgive; that to forgive is a choice, not a feeling. I agree wholeheartedly. But I honestly did not know how to tackle it until I read:

"Love of neighbor assumes the presence of the loving God in the soul of each person and treats each person accordingly. How do I treat Jesus? How does Jesus feel in that soul? How would Jesus like to be treated in the soul of the person in front of us? Jesus would like to be encouraged in that soul. He would like to be strengthened. He would like us to help Him to grow stronger in the soul.... "

So, the other day, when I was speaking to my father on the phone, he told me his wife wanted to speak to me - although it wasn't my first preference - I was able to do it because I knew what to do and how to do it. When she told me that for Lent, she and my father were going to daily Mass, I was able to exhort her, to encourage her, to praise her. I told her that she may find that once Lent is over, she may wish to continue to go, because there is no substitute for the joy, peace and nourishment one gets from hearing the word of God proclaimed, and receiving the precious body and blood of Our Blessed Lord.

M.F.

I have forgiven my siblings, my nieces and nephews, and even my deceased parents for the emotional trauma that I experienced from them most of my life.

Teresa R., TX

I was persecuted about a year ago by a very good friend of mine, or at least I thought she was a good friend. I gave her some information about a group she was involved in that supported anti-life groups. She was calling me names in front of everybody, even my husband. She was just very evil, and it got passed around our school. It was a huge persecution, but I was really able to know in my heart that I was defending the Truth, and I didn't wimp out and cry and apologize for my behavior. I felt so strongly that Our Lord was there with me saying 'you have the grace, do not worry, things will get better.' With that, I was able to withstand that very horrible persecution. In my heart, I have absolutely forgiven her. Even the day that she was calling me all those names (she didn't do it to my face), she called me that evening and was very angry. I remember saying to her, "You have to realize, this isn't anything against you; it is against the company that gives money to another company that performs abortions. I still admire you very much and still consider you to be a good friend of mine." I was able to say something very nice back to her that was extremely genuine. I did not retort back and call her names; whereas in the past I probably would have done that. I felt so strong in my heart knowing that this was the truth and I had to defend the truth. Right now our relationship is different, but I feel that I hold nothing back. I'm very open and when I talk to her I feel so much healing and love. I was able to pray for her at the Day of Renewal, too. I'm sure my prayers helped.

As a result of the persecution I went through, a very dear friend and I were able to form the Little Flower Girls Club at our school, which is a truly Catholic club for girls. The girls are learning about virtues and saints in a fun environment to counteract another group in the upper grades of our school. Since this group exists now, hopefully this other group won't come into our school (a pro-choice group). If that persecution hadn't have happened to me, I probably would not have been so gung-ho, and so on fire to start the Little Flower Girls Club. Through the grace of God and the intercession of St. Therese, and the Blessed Mother, (our patron saints), they have really helped this club be a light in our school.

Doris, Philippines

I still struggle a lot with forgiveness. I can forgive but then I have to ignore the person to avoid committing the same mistake again.

Receiving Forgiveness

Forgive others as Jesus has forgiven you and you will know heaven's peace.
~ Heaven Speaks to Those Who Struggle to Forgive
page 14, Blessed Mother

Mercy and compassion given freely to others delights Me. Forgiveness? I need not even tell you about the happiness that comes to Me when I see souls offering forgiveness to each other.
~Volume 2, September 3, 2003, Jesus

This is what forgiveness is all about... ~Bonnie

Gloria A., NY

I have been able to see with my own eyes, the words Jesus has shared with us; in the messages have come fulfillment with my best friend, Mary, who is dying. There is a statement in *Climbing the Mountain* I use to communicate back and forth with Mary in her dying days. On page 137 in CTM it says, "as you climb the mountain higher and higher toward heaven, our soul becomes stronger and the power of Christ becomes greater. When we begin to disappear then Christ radiates through us." This I have seen. I have witnessed this and it is true. My friend Mary was one of the people I sent the *Volumes* to. She has a hearing impairment and we communicate at a distance through paper and when she's with me, she lip-reads. Well, I sent the books and she was on fire. She started sending them out to everybody. Sometimes she would email me asking, how do you think this person would react to the books?' I told her that it's none of our business. We'll leave that up to Jesus.

Mary has always been a perfectionist. Everything has to be just right. She has brought so much anxiety upon herself, as most perfectionists do. As she questions everything, I tell her she has a St. Thomas Aquinas mind. When I didn't want her to talk anymore, I put my hands over her eyes (she reads lips!). She would laugh and laugh. A few months ago she went to the doctor. When the doctor came in and told her she had a brain tumor, she asked, "How did that get there?" And with the same breath she said, 'God's will be done '(her daughter in law was with her).' Mary only wanted union with whatever God wants. The next thing she said to the doctor, 'if I've done anything to offend you, or have caused you any kind of anxiety, I ask you to forgive me.' Her daughter in law, Cindy, was in awe. Then, she turned to Cindy and said the same thing. When she got home she called every single member of her family asking the same thing. When I heard this, I thought, wow. This is a gift from heaven. So, I went to visit her, as I was afraid I wouldn't get to see her again. When I arrived at her home, I saw the statue of Our Lady next to her, and she looked very different. She pointed to her feet and all around were the *Volumes*. She picked up one of the books and said, this is what has sustained me this last month. She pointed to the statue of Mary and Mary's words from the *Volumes*. As she's talking to me, I realized I'm seeing Jesus. She took my hand and leaned over to me and said, 'if I've ever done anything...' just as she said to all the others. I said to her, 'Mary, I'm sorry but you'll have to forgive me first.' She said, "why?" I said, 'because you've never done anything I'd have to forgive you for.' She threw her head back crying and laughing at the same time.

A few months after seeing Mary, I received a letter from her. Here are some excerpts.

I'd like you to know, Gloria, that every one of my family members has come to visit and express their forgiveness and love. (Gloria's comment: There were some restraints in the family as they don't visit like most families.) It has been the best going away present. It makes my chest swell with such joy and gratitude to Jesus' infinite mercy. Upon learning that Jesus wishes a personal relationship with each of us, that is, I understand He likes us to speak with Him and He will speak as a personal friend. I was finding this difficult due to the distance of God's sovereign immensity, compassion and mercy. So, I spent some time looking to make the vastness of the distance less foreboding. And here is the result, which I share with you for your contemplation. It appears the tumor in my brain is affecting other bodily processes, which we try to assess and cope with day-by-day, moment-by-moment. Grace for the present moment. Jesus loves you and so do I. The problem is how do you talk to God intimately? It seems hard because He is so far above me. The answer is, turn your thoughts from the almighty greatness of God to His infinite love and mercy. Then think about the fact that it is through His mercy that God dwells in us to the gift of His grace. So, you are as close to Him as your own self because He dwells within you. Wow ! How amazing is that? Then it becomes so easy. Just turn inward and speak to Him. It's as easy as thinking. He wants this love and intimacy. When we turn our minds and will to Him, we live in deep intimacy with God and this is the beginning of our heaven, the overture to the symphony.

I read that, walked out to the kitchen and handed it to my husband Jack and said, 'this has been written by a saint.'

Next letter from Mary –

Dear Glo,

Mary can no longer use the computer so she asked me to be her secretary and pass this on to you. I am most grateful to Jesus the Returning King. I continuously ask to be in His presence and He in mine. With His infinite love and desire for all souls to be saved, I trust His merciful love will draw us to

Himself. At this time, my energy diminishes and there are other indications of illness. However, I continue to receive the best of care. There can be no other than the love of Jesus and Mother Mary coming to me. Oh, how I appreciate your prayers and hope you'll continue them. I often expect to be united with you again but (?). I have the longest list of prayer intentions and people for whom I'm praying than I've ever known. I pray for God and Mother Mary to bless them, each and every one. Be assured of my love and prayers. I think our love, Glo, is perhaps being transferred around where most needed. Isn't that all over the world? Mary

This letter is from her kids and her grandkids:

Dear Mom,

We know that you will continue your duty as our mother after you leave this earth with Christ. If you would be so kind to do so, we ask you to request the following favors from Our Lord: All that He knows that we need, show us the way; for spiritual healing; for physical healing; for peace and prosperity. As we go through life we will follow His direction and know He is truly our Father. We ask that He help us to recognize and understand the com- munications from our guardian angels. Mom, you will always be in our hearts, although we will miss you. We know you will be with us and guiding us from your place in heaven.

We love you.

Signed by all children and grandchildren

And, Mary writes back:

To my dear family,

Thank you for writing and requesting my motherly duties after leaving this earth and life. Your welfare has

always been my chief occupation and one that won't end after my death. Furthermore, I expect that in eternity, this will become a supreme joy for me. What happiness to totally rely on the goodness of our all loving Father and then to see Him bless you, each with a gift that will be the best for you. Our triune God and his infinite mercy will not deny such a mothers prayer for her family. I need a favor from all of you, though. In order to take my place before the throne of love, as immediately possible after my death, I depend on your prayers. One of the greatest duties of a child is to honor his mother and father. Most of the time it is a sweet obligation. You have all honored me with your visits and letters and attention in the past weeks and months. It HAS been sweet. And, I thank you for it. Please don't stop. After my death, I will still need you to pray for my path through purgatory, the place of purification, and on to behold the face of God. Remember me in your prayers. And not only will you be keeping our connection with one another strong and vibrant, you will merit the promises God attaches to caring for parents. That is a total present – the hearing of your prayers; treasures in heaven and a long life. Acts 3 4-5 and Exodus 20 verse 12. I love you, each and every one, now and forever.

Note: Mary has since passed away and gone to her heavenly home.

Like any good mother, I forget the mistakes of my children almost immediately. I can help poor sinners to forgive themselves and seek the forgiveness of my Son, a forgiveness that heals and strengthens. Sinners must not be afraid. They must simply close their eyes and say, 'God, I have made mistakes. I'm

sorry. I am Your child, though, and seek to be united to You.' My child, all of heaven weeps for joy when even one soul makes this act of humility and love.
~Volume One, page 92, Blessed Mother

Catherine B. MI

Throughout the divorce, I believe my children (ages 13 and 8) were angry with me. So, I started reading the *Volumes* to them, one letter per night. They faithfully listened and I noticed that my son has forgiven me. He's the older one. It has made a huge difference in our relationship. We have had a family healing reading the *Volumes* together. We understand what Jesus is doing and what He's trying to teach us – how to love and how to forgive.

Estelle C.

In December of 2007 I went to Eucharistic Adoration and a gentleman I usually see at morning mass handed me *Heaven Speaks to Consecrated Souls*. I tried to give it back to him feeling it had nothing to say to me since I'm not a religious sister. He told me it was for me too. Feeling a bit silly, I took it. My curiosity took over and I started to read it. It certainly wasn't what I expected at all. Here was Jesus actually speaking to a contemporary woman. I couldn't put it down. When I saw the other titles I knew I had to learn more. I especially needed to read the booklet on abortion. I'm not the most computer savvy person going but I made it my goal to read this booklet. I couldn't stop crying. It still has the same effect on me today. Even though I'd been to Confession years ago for the first time, I felt as if I was finally really forgiven. After all, didn't Jesus tell me so Himself? Somehow that made it easier to get closer to Him. I'd always felt that I wasn't good enough to have a real relationship with Jesus, that He was only tolerating me. That feeling changed in an instant. The relationship I have with Jesus now just keeps getting stronger each day. I talk to Him all day, sometimes I wonder if I should just be quiet and let Him get a word in edgewise. And He does. Not always, but especially when I'm saying the Rosary or the Stations of the Cross, I suddenly will get a new insight. Often I say, "Is that what You're trying to teach me?' I feel as if I'm His slowest pupil, but He never gives up on me or gets tired of helping me learn. I want so much to put a smile on His beautiful face but He always beats me to it and puts a smile on my face. Sometimes I can feel Him smiling at me.

This relationship is practical as well as spiritual. If I have a problem or a question I'll ask for His input and He never lets me down. Everything from "what's for dinner this week" to how to structure my day. And when I give it all over to His direction it works out seamlessly, no wasted time or effort. Things I used to enjoy hold no interest for me now. It's all about spending each and every day with Him, trying to do His will and bring Him to all the people I meet. He's my first thought in the morning, my last thought at night, and lots of conversations all throughout the day. I haven't been a good sleeper since the abortion in 1980, and for the first time, I no longer dread those sleepless nights. They're not as bad as they used to be, but even now if I'm up it's just more time to speak with Jesus. And it's the perfect time since it's quiet and there aren't any other calls on my time. If I'm feeling particularly down, I'll just ask Him in a rather whining voice that I'm afraid, to hold me and rock me to sleep. I feel like His smallest child and it's the most wonderful feeling. I've never felt so safe, loved and cared for.

There's never a day now that I'm not reading something Anne has written. I just can't get enough. I know He's speaking directly to my heart. Eternity won't be long enough to thank Him for all He's done for me.

Because I love you and because I need your help, I wish to give you the opportunity to

195

*find greater peace in your heart. It is clear
to Me that many suffer from hidden wounds.
The only way for these wounds to heal is for
the carrier of the wound to forgive the one
who inflicted the injury.*
~Heaven Speaks To Those Who Struggle To Forgive,
December 13, 2006, Jesus

Frank

It is indeed in the Name of the Father, and of the Son, and
of the Holy Spirit, that I send these words of peace and hope to
all who read them. If I were to mention all the graces I have
received since discovering the *Volumes* it would contain a
volume itself. For God in his great Divine Mercy has gently
shown me the error of my ways and given me the grace to
reconcile my life back to Him. As I have been forgiven much,
now I love much and have forgiven others much. Welcome to
this journey up the mountain. I pray for you and please pray for
me.

PART FOUR

Sustained Conversions

Sustained Conversions

I will also pursue complete conversion of each of their loved ones. So you see, the souls who serve in this rescue mission as My beloved lay apostles will know peace.
~Volume Nine, May 12, 2005, Jesus

My children, I am anxious that you persevere in your conversions. There are many graces available to you so that you stay this course to holiness.
~Volume Two, September 5, 2003, Blessed Mother

Stacey G., IN

On page 35 of *Volume Two*, Jesus says, "My children, I am with you. You have heard Me say that many times before. Perhaps I have said it so often that you do not really hear it. Today, I want you to both hear these words and understand them. I am with you. Does that mean I watch you from heaven, hoping all goes well with you? Does it mean I gaze out over My whole world, seeing only the large events? No. I am with you. I am with YOU, My child". At the end of the paragraph, He once again repeats, "I am with you".

After reading this paragraph, I went about my day feeling comforted that the Lord is always with me. I was also thinking about service to the Lord and wondering where exactly my place is in all of this. The Volumes have taught me how important it is to become active in spreading His word to others. The Lord's reminder that He is always with me gave me incredible confidence. Still, I wondered what precisely He wanted me to do to help His kingdom. I did not want to let Him down.

While sitting at my computer in the basement, I was feeling "on fire" about the Volumes and excited about passing them on to others. My three-year-old son, Seth, was playing and suddenly brought me a long piece of paper. The paper said, "GOD KNOWS JUST WHERE YOU FIT!" I was completely floored. It especially struck me to see the word YOU in uppercase letters just as it had been written in the book. Furthermore, it was emphasized with the underline. I asked Seth, "Where did you find this?" He gave me a puzzled look and shrugged his shoulders.

At that time, I could not recall ever seeing this piece of paper before. Now that I think about it, I may have some explanation of where it may have come from. There is a bookshelf in my computer room and sometimes the kids play with the books. Well, one of the books is called, *"The Catholic Book of Bible Promises."* This book belongs to my mom. She received it from a friend in 1996 when she went on the "Walk to Emmaus." During the walk, she received many little inspirational notes, books and cards. I am guessing that this note was stuck in the pages of this book and it fell out as Seth played with it. I did not see him playing with the book, but I did have my back turned for a short while. I asked my mom about the note, but she received so many on the Walk that she could not remember this particular one.

For me, where the note came from is really beyond the point. I realize it did not magically appear and that it must have come from somewhere. Regardless of its origin, I believe that the Lord used my son to find the note and hand it to me at that point in time when the *Volumes* were so heavy on my mind. I think that He does this for us at many times during our life...at this point in time, I just happened to be paying attention!

This note means a lot to me and I keep it on the dresser mirror in my bedroom, as a daily reminder that God has a plan for me. He knows just where I fit! Most importantly, He wants me to *trust* Him and not worry. I feel very thankful to the Lord for His encouragement and His unique way of delivering this message to me.

Barbara S. CA

After seeing Anne speak in California almost two years ago, I began saying the rosary daily and have found it provides a structure to communicate with God, Mary and the saints. It also provides me feelings of peace and relaxation.

"Let nothing stand in the way of your conversion to silence. It is there you will find Jesus."
~Volume One, page 86, Blessed Mother

Terry S., PA

I am blind in one eye and my other eye is deteriorating. But the amazing thing is I have a cross in the blind eye. I literally see a cross when I look at people, right through their face. I've been to five doctors and they can't figure it out. I spoke with a very holy priest and he said some of my greatest joy and peace are going to come from the cross. In the monthly message a few months ago, one line caught my eye. Jesus said, "I arrange all things in your life." After reading that the peace and joy set in. I know this is from God. It's not a mistake. He provides you with everything you need when He gives you a cross. It's Divine Will. This is what He wants for you and we need to be at peace.

Catherine B.

I work for the Dept. of Human Services and deal with the worst of the worst situations that arise in our state. Everyone wonders how I get my work accomplished. I tell them you have to let God take control. Now, they are calling me the "Let go and let God" lady. I was reading *Volume Seven* and the messages from St. Therese of the Little Flower. The friend who gave me the *Volumes* mentioned there was a shrine not far from my work. He had gone over there one day and looked around. I was reading about the shrine and that there is an Adoration chapel there. I go at least 3-4 times a week at lunchtime. I have developed a relationship with St. Therese.

Cecilia M. CA

During a time of recovery after a stroke in March of 2006, a friend gave me *Climbing the Mountain* saying she needed the book returned in two days. She wanted to know my discernment of the messages. The truth is I could not put the book down and finished it in a day and a half. Since that time, I have read all of the "Anne" books, *Volumes* and leaflets. Each month I download the message given by Our Lord. I reread this message to check if I'm living His words for the month.

Many times I feel the need to reread a *Volume*, one of the messages or a specific e-book, and there will be the answer to something I may be struggling with. Here is a recent example: My charisms are intercessory prayer and teaching. I was struggling with a situation in our youth program. One day as I was searching for some papers, *Volume Nine - Angels* was laying open between a stack of paperwork. As I read Sept 3, 2004 from Jesus...there was my answer: "Any task entrusted to you has also been entrusted to one or more angels, who are assigned to assist you. You see that you are never alone." Sometimes we 'know' these things but we forget them and we need these little concrete reminders from Our Lord that heaven is with us and we are truly working with heaven.

> *Remember that your brothers and sisters*
> *in heaven walked your paths of conversion.*
> ~Volume One, page 94, Jesus

Chris O.

In 2001, I had reached a time in my life when I needed to find the God I had learned about as a child: God our Loving Father, Protector, and Healer. And Jesus who had promised that he would always be with us.

Responsibilities were weighing heavily on me. Some of those were common ones: raising a family, working long hours at our jobs, and taking additional work home. Also contributing to the pressures of daily life was the lasting effect of my brother's sudden death in 1994 on my emotional health, and becoming the guardian for his two children, who had come to live with my family. My brother's children were age 10-months and two and a half years old at the time of his death. We brought them to our home fourteen months later. They had been living in squalor, were emotionally scarred, malnourished and ill. A private investigator had been unable to find them before answered prayers and a Good Samaritan had located them.

Doctors, psychologists, social workers, and teachers explained that many years of treatment would be required to help these children with their deficiencies. And so it has been, and continues to be, a challenge. Only with God's help could we have continued to face the challenges and reap any success.

During the first weekend of October 2004, my husband and I were privileged to attend another Marian Conference. After we had selected our seats, I went to locate the room organized for selling religious articles and books. I found a table with a sign hanging over it and some little books piled on top of it. The books were small and different colors. They were numbered, strangely and simply named *Volumes*. What were these *Volumes* about, I wondered? Then, I noticed the books referenced a woman, mother of six (I had been raising six), who had written down messages from Jesus. The cost per book was only $5.

At this point in my spiritual journey, I was able to admit with confidence and faith that I had seen, heard, and experienced amazing evidence of God's presence in our lives, and how He used others to accomplish His work. I believed in miracles, I believed in Marian Visitation, and I believed in the Charisms of the Holy Spirit. I also believed in Satan and exorcism. However, a mother of six children, writing volumes of messages from Jesus? I <u>could not</u> rationalize this phenomenon. It seemed more like an introduction to a type of New Age dimension of spiritual enlightenment. Because I believe that one can never be too cautious, I was skeptical, guarded, and walked away from the display. However, shortly after, I thought to myself that $5 would not be too much of a loss, if it all turned out to be just a hoax. I only purchased the brown book, *Volume One*, and then eagerly attended the conference.

I felt compelled to read the other *Volumes*. First I read through them quickly, then, again, slowly. I was driven to share the *Volumes* with everyone I could think of so that no one would be left out.

I work in the field of accounting and have an analytical mind. I believe Jesus spoke the words. Each time I have an opportunity to read a monthly message, which I don't always have access to on the first day of the month, I am amazed by its content and relevance in my life!

It saddens me to think of the many individuals who turn away from the opportunity to know and follow our Sweet Jesus! I know, through this experience, that I belong to God. My longings for Jesus have grown even stronger after reading the *Volumes* and monthly messages.

I feel that I have stepped out from a false world into a world of Truth. My life has been blessed! There is no turning back! No one will ever convince me that God does not answer prayer. My prayer to find those who Jesus works through has surpassed my desires. Jesus is with us, just as He had promised in scripture, and just as He continues to remind us through the Volumes and messages. I believe that Heaven is sending us an incredibly awesome gift through Anne!

In days past, perhaps you conversion would be more gentle and leisurely. I do not will that now and its is not what I require.
~Volume Two, Sept. 1, 2003, Jesus

Debbie J., CA

In December 2004, I asked my sister what she would like for her birthday. She recently read the Volumes, so she told me that for her birthday gift she would like me to read the Volumes. I ordered the whole set and once I started reading, I couldn't put them down. I just knew in my soul these messages were from Heaven and that Jesus was speaking directly to my soul. That was the beginning of my conversion to really live my Catholic faith and to start serving the Kingdom instead of the world. I now attend daily Mass, go to confession monthly, and try to go to Adoration weekly--and I belong to a wonderful Lay Apostle group!

I still face many challenges and probably more, but now I take all of my problems and worries to Jesus, Mary, the Saints and Angels. I thank God for His mercy in calling me to this mission--and I thank my sister for the most wonderful gift she could have ever given me!

Denise R.

The beginning of my call into this apostolate is very much like the beginning of the Gospel of Jesus Christ. First, Jesus and Mary called me to Medjugorje and before I even arrived there, this apostolate came into my life. My first encounter was with an audio CD of a Eucharistic Day of Renewal with Anne, and I kept hearing Jesus tell me that He loved me. Next, I bought the *Volumes* and the same thing happened. I felt like I had found the most incredible audio books ever! I heard Him speak to me every time I opened the books and all the while I felt I was getting personal instruction that was written just for me. Since this time, I have grown in awareness of the presence of the Blessed Trinity and the Blessed Mother. I have grown to love the Word of God and have been led to a deeper understanding of Scripture.

Before this conversion, I thought I was near the top of the mountain of holiness. After reading the *Volumes*, I began to roll down the mountain, like a huge ball of mud, sticks and stones. As the ball rolled down the hill, the debris began to fly off and I became uncovered. Now I have found myself at the foot of the mountain, naked and climbing slowly. The wonderment of it all is awesome and the people that are encouraging me along the way have been heavenly. I find that as I climb in my nakedness, a light has begun to clothe me.

The following testimony is from one of the most loving, kind and faith filled women I know, with the best biscotti recipe ever.~Bonnie

Frances L., CO

In November 2005, I called Father Lawrence Malcolm at St. Daniel the Prophet Parish in Chicago, which is the current headquarters for the Ministry of Praise. I needed some questions answered and during the conversation, Father offered me Sister Charla's phone number. I put off this call until January 5, 2006, because I needed time to build up courage. I read an old interview of hers many times and intended to ask her for an updated interview. I never got the interview. Instead, Sister Charla immediately began to tell me about the *Volumes*. She was so excited about them. She told me to get a set and gave me the contact information for *Direction for Our Times*. She made sure I understood that I did not call on my own. She assured me the Holy Spirit made me call her. At the end of our conversation, she told me to order another set for my Pastor. After saying our goodbyes, I marveled at the fact that Sister talked to me as though she knew me all my life. I chuckled to myself recalling how nervous I was about calling her. She is a sweetheart, I thought as I relayed her message to my husband, Ralph. I was still processing Sister Charla's suggestions when his enthusiasm surprised me. He said, "Let's get a set of the Volumes". I will always be thankful to God for having made that call to Sister Charla. It changed our lives. When the Volumes arrived, we devoured them. Soon we bought extras and gave many books to our priests, relatives, friends and fellow-parishioners. On June 1, 2006, Ralph and I started a lay apostles of Jesus Christ, the Returning King prayer meeting in our home with our daughter Suzette and her husband, Kenton, joining us. Soon our friends, Bev and Ed Rios not only joined us but also arranged a meeting with our Pastor, who very kindly agreed to let us meet in the Church. Before talking to Sister Charla, my heroine, I was afraid to evangelize. I was fearful of telling a person something wrong. I also thought once you evangelize you must take on the teaching of that person for life. Jesus tells us in *Volume Ten* (P. 17), "Often you are like a farmer sowing seeds. I, Myself, must reap the harvest." He also says, "Use My words...Spread them everywhere." With these words, He has replaced my fear with courage and made me eager to spread His messages. I pray for His guidance before and while witnessing then leave them with a *Volume* to read. The *Volumes* have changed my thinking and deepened my prayer life. From early on, what impressed me was how the Volumes and the other writings verify all I have ever been taught as a Catholic through the Church and the Scriptures. What is awe-inspiring is the discovery that God is talking directly to me. It is simultaneously a humbling and an uplifting experience to realize the intensity of His love for me. Each book increases my love for Him.

Since reading these books, I have gotten closer to the Holy Trinity, the Blessed Mother and the saints. Eucharistic Adoration has become sweeter and soul penetrating, a true blessing to me. When the Lord nudges me to witness to someone, He fills me with His joy and enthusiasm. He has led me to share His words with many people in our Church, restaurants and the hospital, even in an airplane. The monthly Messages are my classrooms to holiness. I am a breast cancer survivor, praise God. However, I still have many health issues, some of which rank from painful to extremely painful. Ralph had to remind me at first to offer up all my sufferings large and small for the Rescue Mission. The books taught me how important this practice is to Jesus. The good news is suffering allows me to stay in close contact with the Lord. I cry out to Him loudly for strength through my painful attacks. When it is over, I sit quietly and gratefully before the Lord and bask in His healing touch. How blessed I am along with my fellow lay apostles to be part of Jesus' mission.

As I travel this heavenward trail with all its surprising twists and turns, I know the Lord will sustain me with spiritual food for the journey, just as He is right now with all of Anne's writings.

Judy M., FL

I first heard about the *Volumes* from a friend discerning to become a nun. We met in Medjugorje. One night she gave me *Volume One* to read. I started reading and knew in my heart the messages were true. But, I told her I couldn't read anymore because I wasn't ready. I had so much going on in my life. I told her at some point, when it was right, God would send them to me. For about a year, I thought about them. One day I was about to order the *Volumes* online and didn't have my credit card to fulfill paying for the order. God's hand was in that because what happened was a couple of weeks later I went to a Magnificat and Sandy T. was there. She gave testimony about Medjugorje and then everyone attending the Magnificat was given a Volume. So I thought, ok, now it's time. God's throwing them in my lap and I need to do this. I went to the

Catholic Marketing Trade Show because I run my parish gift shop. While I was there, I was thinking I needed to find these books (*Volumes*). It was the first trade show I had ever been to. As I was walking down the aisles, I was thinking how God is always so good to me. I then see this whole entire booth set up with the *Volumes,* all of them. As I said, I didn't know much about them, but knew I had to be involved in this.

I got two cases of the *Volumes* into the parish. The first four sets of shipments never made it into the parish store. I told people about them and it was like the book mobile in my car. The shipment would come in, and people would track me down and ask if I had the *Volumes.* So, they were selling out of the back of my car for months. Literally, it was about six months before they got into the parish store. One woman in particular in the parish, whom I met about ten years ago and knew from the parish, came to me one day and said, " I have to talk to you. I need you to start a prayer group." I explained that she would have to talk to Father John before starting a prayer group because you have to have his approval. I asked her what the focus was and she informed me that she was buying cases from *DFOT* and handing out *Volumes.* As a real estate agent, she gave one to everybody who bought a house from her, and she also distributed *Volumes* in pews of other parishes. Her example prompted us to give away two *Volumes* asking people to turn someone else on to these and keep passing them out. That's how it grew in our parish. We prayed on it first, too. I told her I don't do anything unless I pray on it. I asked her what she wanted me to do. She said she wanted me to lead it because I have the ability and personality to do it. So she saw Father John, but he wasn't completely sold on the mission and didn't quite believe in it. Father John is my spiritual director, so I was able to talk to him. He trusted me and so he allowed it. He even came to the *Mist of Mercy* screening one night. He said everything that Anne says is true and nothing that we don't know. That's the point. That's how you know. He said it was very comforting. I've shown it four times in our parish and so many loved coming because they were raised thinking of purgatory as a scary place. Then they bring others to it.

The very first meeting had sixteen people. It happened to be a feast day. We always pray the Luminous Mysteries on feast days. We want people to meditate on them. Before we started praying, I explained that the beauty of our starting that night was that it was the date Pope John Paul II became pope many years ago. It was significant because he is the one that gave us the Luminous Mysteries. I felt, at this point, it was a nod from God. After we were done praying the mysteries, everyone was moved to tears. We all felt so emotionally filled. One of the women stepped forward from our charismatic prayer group. She had a vision of the Blessed Mother with her hands out smiling upon us saying 'thank you' during the rosary. Since we had been struggling to know what we were doing, this was our Yes. After the first year we grew to 35 members. The beautiful thing was that Father John had to hear confession a lot more because people were lining up regularly and people were going to morning mass when maybe they hadn't before.

Gail P., TX

My son Steve, husband and father of five, read *Volume Two* and took to heart the suggestion of a daily visit before the Blessed Sacrament.

During his first visit to the chapel, which he fit in between his two jobs, Steve was so exhausted he fell asleep and had this very "vivid and unforgettable dream." He saw Jesus with several of His friends, walking up the road toward him. Following them in the distance was a multitude. One of the apostles must have said something very funny because Jesus responded by throwing His head back and laughing heartily. Then when passing in front of Steve, Jesus turned and gave him a big wink.

It has been my belief that whenever Jesus makes His Presence known, or a "connection" with someone, it is in a manner compatible to their personality. When my son described this experience to me, it made sense as Steve loves to laugh and joke. He also wondered if there were any pictures of Jesus laughing, as he could not remember ever seeing one.

Steve also teaches religion classes to the children at the local parish of St. Michael's in McKinney, TX. Several weeks after this "encounter" in the chapel, he was browsing the internet for pictures of Jesus to give to the kids. He was so elated when he came across a sketch of Jesus that depicted Him exactly as he saw Him in his "dream." What a confirmation!

Needless to say, Steve has read and reread all of the *Volumes* and has purchased and passed out countless books to family, friends, and strangers alike. Such an evangelizer! (I think he was "called" on the road).

"Truly there is a great storehouse of graces for these days so be certain to always petition heaven, particularly for conversions."
~Volume Seven, July 6, 2004, page 7
St. Therese, The Little Flower

Gina P., MI

About 19 years ago my husband and I accepted Jesus Christ as our Lord and Savior. From then on we attended only non-denominational Christian churches. We took many Bible study classes throughout the years, and we learned a lot. Still, we both always felt like something was missing from our faith. Then one day about 2 years ago I came into my home and heard the sound of the television in my bedroom. I had accidentally left it on before leaving the house. (Something I have never done before or since.) When I went into the bedroom to turn it off I noticed there was a woman speaking about her experience in heaven with Jesus. It was Anne. Normally I am very cynical of such things and I would have turned the television right off.

But this time I felt certain that she was telling the truth. I just knew she had been with Jesus and that He had showed her heaven. After the television show ended, I ordered her book, *Mist of Mercy*. I loved it so much that I immediately ordered all eight of the Volumes next. Again, God gave me the grace to see that the words spoken to this prophet are indeed words given to her by the Lord Himself. I can't even describe the peace and the joy I have received from reading the books. I can honestly say that they have had just as much of a transforming power on me as the Bible has. And there are no other books I have ever read that I can say that about. In fact, as a result of Anne's writings, both my husband and I have converted to Catholicism. Words cannot describe how happy we are in the Catholic Church. We feel like we have finally found the one thing missing from our faith since we gave our lives to Christ all those years ago. And for the first time in our lives we look forward to going to church each week.

Holly K., IN

I have started praying the Rosary. I had never done that before. I've been going to confession – I try to do that every month. I never saw the importance of it all. I felt I didn't need to go to confession to have my sins forgiven, at least that's what I told myself. I didn't really understand when Jesus talks about receiving graces by going to confession and why we should do that. But now I have a better understanding of it. I spend a lot more time in prayer. Every day I make a commitment to spend time with God. I understand now that I have to keep up my end of the relationship. I used to, and this is big for me, I used to not pray about certain things because I viewed it as wasting God's time when He has all these other people's problems. But, through the (*DFOT*) books, I've learned He wants to listen to me. He wants me to bring everything to Him. I used to think, 'why tell Him that, He knows everything. If He wants something to happen, it will happen.' Now I know He wants a relationship with me. He loves me. He wants to share my worries and concerns. He wants to walk along side me. By praying every day, I invite Him into my life to walk beside me. I've always felt I was a spiritual person. My parents always took us to church every week. I always went to church every week, even after I moved out. But, I didn't understand that relationship with Jesus. It's like we have become active participants with Christ and His plan.

Judy, FL

The first day we had a Lay Apostle meeting, we were in the middle of the rosary, in the second decade, and the Blessed Mother came to me and said she was very pleased with the lay apostles. When we went back to gather around together, (I'm not the type of person who just can say what happened-it was just so awesome) I told the Blessed Mother there was no way I could do this and to please help me. My heart was beating about a hundred miles an hour. All of a sudden I just started saying (to the group) the Blessed Mother came to me and she is very pleased. I said it to Judy (M.) and Judy went, "what, what, what? Wait, everyone stop." She told me to say it again, which was even harder. So, I told everybody. It was just a beautiful, beautiful moment.

Margaret A., FL

I was introduced to the books of Anne in Louisiana at a Magnificat conference. I was so touched by *Volume One* telling of the power of prayer. I read most of the *Volumes* and then purchased *Climbing The Mountain*. I attend a Charismatic Prayer Meeting on Thursday evenings. At this meeting attendees are asked to share a testimony or a book they have read. I knew this was it! It was difficult for me to condense part of this book to 30 minutes or less, but after prayer to the Holy Spirit, I did it, picking out parts of our climb and how easy it is to fall off of the mountain. Months went by and I then read *Mist of Mercy*. Wow! I was so moved by the section on Spiritual Warfare, as I had just recognized, through the Holy Spirit, an incident in my life where Satan had seduced me! I thank God, Jesus, Mary and the Holy Spirit for leading me to Anne's works.

"There are many conversion powers attached to these words so see that you spread them to the best of your ability, following His lead and direction."
~Volume Seven, July 14, 2004, page 34, St. Damien

Madeline D. FL

My sister Christine attended St. Gregory Catholic College in the late 60's. The end result was she left the Catholic faith. I have prayed for her for years. Not until I joined the lay apostles did I see the fruit of my prayers. With my promise to Jesus and Mary and following the guidelines laid out by Jesus, in less than one year my sister came back to the faith in a big way. She says the rosary and goes to mass daily. She also attended a large Catholic Conference in California. She did all this in less than 30 days. He did not stop there. He has increased my husband's faith so much that we go to mass daily and pray the rosary together. He has no problem telling anyone who will listen how wonderful the Catholic faith is. We serve an awesome God. He promised if I said YES to Him, He would take care of my family.

Rebecca B., CO

Being a mother of five has its sufferings and challenges – picking up the cross and walking with Christ. I started reading Anne's messages on the *DFOT* website. I looked for a prayer group in Colorado, but there wasn't any at that time. I begged the Lord for someone to pray with as I was in great need of a prayer group. A year later I checked again and there was a name (Mary), so I called her. In our conversation we talked about adoration and the parishes we were in. It ended up she was a great prayer warrior in adoration with my sister. We laughed so hard at what a golden thread God was weaving in His tapestry. After this, while at church in Denver, I received one of the *Volumes* from a priest, *Volume Two*. I knew that was confirmation from God that I was on the right path. I thank God so much for confirming this was part of His journey for me. I've been with the prayer group since.

Cheryl D., FL

When my dear friend first told me about the messages an American mother was receiving from Jesus, I admit I was skeptical. But, since this is the same friend who visited Medjugorje and told me of the miracles she witnessed there, who has often referred me to books of greater spiritual understanding and prayers that have changed my life, I listened and agreed to watch a video made by this woman named simply "Anne."

I watched the video as Anne was interviewed by the media. During the course of the video, the face of Anne was never shown. I listened to what she had to say, and was profoundly moved. Anne's interview gave me a glimpse into the life of a modern, humble woman, who was chosen to receive simple yet profound, life-changing messages from the heavens and to eventually share them with the world. I saw a woman who lived with the heartache of single parenthood, disease and an ordinary daily existence. I was surprised that if the messages she was receiving were true, why would Jesus pick this woman to receive them? But as I listened to her testimony, I heard more of what Jesus was saying to her. I heard Jesus' messages and guidance for her and knew it could be for me. I felt drawn into the text of what was said.

The messages were filled with love and light and a gentleness that could really only be from a heavenly source. And I believed.

Joy D., FL

I come to the monthly lay apostle prayer group for the Good Lord and Blessed Mother to guide me to raise my three girls in our faith, to help me make good decisions and keep them safe. Our prayer group forces me to be quiet in prayer and listen to Our Lord for answers. I am more at peace knowing that I have prayed for family and friends.

In your time of service, you will come across many a soul who is in need of conversion."
~Volume Nine, August 30, 2004, page 19, Jesus

Julie

I am a college professor at a small Catholic Benedictine school and have summers off from my classes. Usually, I spend the time preparing for the next academic year, working on projects around the house or doing things with my family. Now that my children are teenagers and have their own busy schedules, and my husband is retired, I wondered how I would spend the summer of 2008. When a dear friend told me about the books, I ordered them that day... all of them. God, in His goodness, led me on a retreat throughout the summer as I read and reflected upon every message in every Volume. Such peace.... strength....comfort.

My husband returned to weekly adoration.... I make regular visits to our adoration chapel on campus and attend daily mass as often as possible. My 16-year-old daughter reads the Volumes before she goes to sleep. I share the messages with my son, who is now away at college and struggling to find himself as a Christian in a secular world. He thinks God is calling him to the priesthood, but he's fighting it. I know his future is in God's Hands, and that Jesus is with him every step of the way. I no longer feel apologetic when I put my children first, or shy away from proclaiming God's mercy and goodness to others. I'm able to connect with our students on a deeper level and see

Christ in each of them. I see myself in Anne... in her struggles, challenges, questions and sense of "I'm not worthy". But isn't that the miracle? None of us is worthy, yet all are equally and unconditionally loved. Jesus knew that it would be easier for some of us to identify with a "regular" person. Although I have read a lot of books about the saints and have learned a lot, I never really felt as though their lives mirrored mine. Consequently, I was never quite sure how to "live that life" on a daily basis. Jesus obviously understands that feeling and cares enough to help us in a very concrete and direct way. Again and again, He reaches down to us, with outstretched arms.

With a very humble and grateful heart, I thank Anne for being open to the Holy Spirit, and I thank the Lord for His never-ending graces. Each day is a new journey, one step closer to our Heavenly home!

Kathleen M., FL

When I first heard of Anne and the lay apostle ministry, I was very skeptical. Who is this lady and what is a locutionist? What does the Pope think of this and does he approve? I'm an old fashioned Catholic and I need the okay from the church and the Pope to feel comfortable becoming a part of any ministry.

Answer to the questions regarding Anne, the locutionist, and the Pope:

There were two things that had a huge impact on my comfort level regarding this ministry. First was a conversation on a Catholic radio station. A question was posed to a priest asking why so many people are receiving messages now from Jesus and how the Catholic Church responds to it. The priest said, "Jesus is reaching out to so many people because we are needed to help Him do His work on earth." The Catholic Church simply cannot respond to every single person who has been called to receive messages because there are so many who have been given this gift and because it is a very long process to figure things out. The important thing is to look at the messages. If they go against the Catholic faith, it is a red flag. If the messages coincide with our beliefs, there should not be any hesitations." If you look at the messages Anne has received, they all coincide with Catholic belief.

A friend of mine is friends with a priest in Ireland where Anne lives. He said that the Irish priests are the most skeptical bunch of priests you will ever meet. If the priests in Ireland believe in Anne then you should feel comfortable with her, too.

Most of all, the messages Anne has received and the ministry guidelines that we are asked to follow all go along with the Catholic faith and provide immense peace. Praying the rosary, the allegiance prayer, sitting in front of the Blessed Sacrament, going to confession are all things that the Catholic Church encourages us to do anyway. Most of all, it provides us with peace and insight and love for Jesus. It brings us closer to Jesus and improves our relationship with Him. We are all very blessed to be able to be a part of this ministry and have Anne's deep commitment and faith in following Jesus' directions.

You will witness many conversions through your service to Me during this time of graces into the world.
~Volume Ten, Oct. 6, 2004, Jesus

Moira, Argentina

When I read the messages I felt like they confirmed what I knew already: that heaven is on earth so to speak, not somewhere remote and disconnected but right here and now, interacting, caring and feeling!

Bill C., NY

I was raised Catholic in the Chicago area. During my teenage years, through college, and as a young adult, I stopped going to Mass and fell away from the Faith. I lost confidence and had too many doubts about the Church. In 1973 I married a woman who had been raised Catholic, too. When our first child was born five years after we married, we came back to the Church mainly for our daughter. She attended Catholic school and we all went to Mass every Sunday. Our second child was born with autism and we made sure he was also raised in the Church. All this time my feelings about the church never really changed. I wasn't against our faith. I just didn't have the enthusiasm. Then one night back in 2002, I was watching late night TV and ran across a show by Focus TV. I saw a presentation about a guy named Howard Storm who had a near death experience. It was very powerful for me and very believable. He wrote a book called My Descent into Hell. The book was very scary, especially if you were away from the Church. I kept watching Focus as they brought on other people, and Anne came along with her story about the locutions. I sent for the books and they really got to me. I honestly believed Jesus, God the Father, and the Virgin Mary were talking to me. I have a couple of advanced degrees, and you can challenge it all intellectually. Either it gets you or it doesn't. Either you believe or you don't. It brought me back to the Church. I am trying to do all the lay apostle things – I'm a little weak on a couple of them – but I definitely don't miss Mass anymore. I'm going to confession every couple of months. I drop by the church a couple of times a week, I even enjoy going to daily Mass. It's the thing that drives me. It has become the focus of my life. Every morning I say my prayers. That's where I am now. My attitude is so completely different. I actually love everybody, no matter how crazy they are! And, they're all genuine feelings. I realize how far I have to go which stops me from saying something about somebody else. My whole attitude has changed.

Catherine N.

In 2006, I was talking with a friendly repairman about the Blessed Mother. Afterward, he went out to his truck and proceeded to give me a copy of *Volume One*: *Direction for Our*

Times. For two years, that little maroon book sat in my bedside nightstand. One night, while praying a novena to St. Padre Pio, a feeling came over me to pull out Anne's book and read it. When I came across a quote by St. Pio, I immediately knew it was him who led me to this amazing little book. St. Pio, in all his love and kindness, wanted me to read it, to be blessed by it and to be changed by its messages. I am now reading *Volume Three* and there are no words to describe the wonderful feelings I get when I read God the Father, Jesus and our Blessed Mother's beautiful, loving words. They soothe my soul. I weep with tears of awe and joy. At times, I feel so full of Their infinite and powerful love for me, I literally have to stop myself while reading in order to take it all in. Anne's books have changed me in that I've learned to request the help of our Blessed Mother, the angels and saints on a daily basis. They truly are our heavenly friends and I realize how much they can guide, bless and protect my family. I'm trying hard to live as the messages request.

Maribeth A., Philippines

I am a 52-year-old mother with three sons. I was a member of the Independent church and converted to Catholicism when I studied in a Catholic High School (Secondary School) in 1968. Jesus has been a friend to me since I was eight years old. I had a strict mother, with all her praises given to my eldest sister who was consistently an honor student and received awards every year. It was my frustration. I didn't receive any awards during my school days even though I tried my best to study hard. I was an above average student. I tried to win the recognition of my mother by helping her do the household chores. I helped her by washing and ironing the clothes and cleaning the house. When our relatives or her friends visited her, she was very proud of me because of all the work I'd been doing at home. My happiness couldn't be contained in that moment. I had a very simple ambition in life, to finish my studies so I could help my parents. I did not dream of becoming somebody someday or travel to different places. To me it didn't matter, as long as I lived a simple, clean and peaceful life.

One day, while surfing the internet, I was surprised to find the website of *Direction for Our Times*. When I read: "*You are here because He has led you to us. Welcome,*" I knew God led me to this site because I'd been asking Him for my mission. I emailed to the US *DFOT* office to ask how I could get a copy of a "Volume," and to my surprise our uncle and aunt who came back from the U.S. to the Philippines to live told me they were familiar with the name, Anne. When they went home to their province of Pangasinan, my husband accompanied them. My husband called me up and said that my uncle gave him the Volumes written by Anne, the lay apostle. When I got hold of the book, I looked to see where it was published. I was so happy to know the books had been published in the Philippines since they were introduced in 2005. God revealed to me my new mission which is an extension of my Divine Mercy mission, and that is to introduce the *Volumes* and invite parishioners to be His lay apostles and later promote it to other parishes. This was the first time I totally committed myself to God. As I recite the Morning Prayer every day, I tell Jesus that I will commit myself to His mission until my last day here on earth. I was able to distribute several copies of the *Volumes,* and many responded already by becoming lay apostles. I thank the Lord for helping me in this mission. I've read all the books of Anne including *Climbing the Mountain, Mist of Mercy* and *Serving in Clarity.* God speaks to me through these books. Now, I'm totally changed. I went to confession after committing the heaviest sins in my life. There was a time I felt God abandoned me. But now I have returned to God's embrace and my life will never be the same again. Every month when I receive the message from Jesus through Anne, I translate it into our own language and I read this in our monthly lay apostles prayer meeting. I asked for forgiveness from my sisters and relatives whom I offended and hurt. I am now a committed Catholic willing to embrace my faith and love for Jesus. I surrender everything to God and give my full trust to Him. I am now sharing this love with everyone I meet. I am more compassionate and sensitive to their needs. God is speaking to me through the messages. Now, I have found what I've been searching for, for such a long time. It is the joy and peace within my heart through the love of Jesus, my Friend and Savior.

"We seek to be united to Jesus in our daily work and through our vocations, in order to obtain graces for the conversion of sinners."
~Heaven Speaks to Those Who do not Know Jesus, page 18, Anne, a lay apostle

Martha L. OK

My younger sister told me about *Climbing the Mountain* in September of 2007. I have had a pretty good prayer life for many years, but had in the previous two years I had been very undisciplined about sitting down every day for time with Our Lord. In October of 2005, we lost our dad, followed by losing Mother seven months later. They had been married 65 years and had a profound effect on all of their children's lives. Losing them had rocked me hard - I was so glad they were on their way to their reward and no longer suffering, but I missed them so! In those two years since, I had prayed every day, but my prayer life was dry and, as I said before, very undisciplined.

I was searching for a way back to a stronger discipleship, when Anne's book came into my life. I nearly read the book in one sitting. My sister and I talked about the book constantly and that lead to my ordering several more copies to give away. I sent one to an older sister and gave another to a friend who was considering going to RCIA classes. (My friend later told me that reading parts of the book in my living room one afternoon gave her courage to go to RCIA classes and that sharing the book with her husband and son over the next month convinced them to attend with her. They were all accepted into the church at the next Easter Vigil. I was the family's sponsor.)

Shortly after reading the first book, I read *Mist of Mercy*. It was a joy to read especially considering the loss of my parents. I remember one morning during my prayer time having a vision of my parents walking hand in hand out of the mist and into Heaven. I wish I could convey how comforted I was. During this same time I started attending weekly Eucharistic Adoration and fell in love all over again with Jesus. Attending monthly Confession rather than my normal yearly Confession has also enriched my prayer life. My priest calls it a "spiritual tune up." Is he ever right! Many of the sins in my life held me back spiritually, but now I have finally been healed.

Remembering to see Jesus in those I meet everyday gives me the grace to be kinder to strangers. Don't get me wrong. I still lose my temper, but not nearly as much. The apostleship has made a profound effect on my life in all ways.

I could go on and on. It's funny how paying attention to the nudging of the Holy Spirit causes you to do things you never thought you'd have the strength to do. I have been thinking about my Mother all evening. My husband's elderly aunt died today, and I have not only said prayers for her, but for her children who sat at her bedside the past two days. I was given the privilege of being at my Mother's bedside during her final week of life. The first time I said the Divine Mercy Chaplet was at her bedside with these two same sisters that I wrote about earlier. That was both the best and hardest week of my life. I think my Mother through a nudge from the Holy Spirit, got me out of bed tonight to finally write this testimony. Thank you for giving me the opportunity.

Mary K., CO

Since becoming a lay apostle, my faith is stronger. I want to get involved more since I became a lay apostle. I want to go to the finance meetings at our church. I want to see more people coming into our church. I want to help get our Adoration chapel built.

If they can accept the crosses in their lives, I can make them saints.
~Climbing the Mountain, page 26, Jesus

Mary K., FL

My friend Barbara and I are involved in making rosaries for the missions and soldiers in combat. We wanted to start a group here in our area. So, of course, we needed to find some interested people. "Aha, here's a lead," I thought to myself when I saw the notice in the church bulletin. Surely they (the Ft. Myers lay apostle prayer group) will be interested in making rosary beads for the missions; after all, they are already devoted to the Rosary. I couldn't find anyone better or more perfectly suited, so perhaps I'll recruit some of them." BUT guess who was "recruited?" Or was it perhaps the Blessed Mother in action? The group welcomed me warmly and when they told me about Anne and the *Volumes*, I couldn't read fast enough and had to consciously slow myself down so I could absorb, reflect on and enjoy the beauty of the messages. Such love and peace I haven't known for a while. How come we so easily lose sight of all that is so precious and readily available? This is surely a way to deepen my spiritual life. And yes! I will work toward being a soldier for His Kingdom. As directed, I will follow.

Susanne B.

As a youngster, I was taught obedience and fidelity to the Church. Strongly drawn to the faith, I often attended daily Mass even as a teenager, following the priest's every move with a missalette, learning as much as I could about it. Then as adults, my husband and I rarely missed Sunday Mass and attended daily Mass as our work schedules permitted. Yet, something was missing. I participated in Church life in many ways - as Eucharistic Minister, CCD teacher, RCIA presenter and RENEW coordinator, among a few. Something was still missing. I became interested in Divine Mercy and read and prayed, sensing an increased closeness to Jesus. After a time, my husband joined me in Divine Mercy devotions. I didn't know what else I could do within my Church to develop a relationship. Sometimes I would be envious of Protestant affirmations of a personal relationship with Jesus. Then someone told me about Anne coming to Medway, Massachusetts. It's a town not far away from where I live. Because of the enthusiasm of the person relaying the information, my husband and I decided to attend. We even brought someone along with us. Our lives were changed forever.

Jesus has come into our lives in a powerful way; letting us know how much He loves us. This closeness has enriched our devotions, including Divine Mercy. Our ministries have been impacted, and given us a new peace. Even in the face of these grave economic times, we know we are God's children, in His loving care. As we pray fervently for our children who are separated from the Church, we know they are in His loving care.

Pauline S., FL

I first became a follower of Jesus Christ the Returning King in August 2008, after my brother in Birmingham, England sent the book *Climbing the Mountain* by Anne, a lay apostle to me here in South Florida. I simply could not put that book down once I began reading it. Since then I have been receiving the messages in emails and found it has helped to strengthen my faith in Jesus and Mary.

Denise V., PA

The message of the lay apostles of Jesus Christ the Returning King came about at the most appropriate time in my life. It began with the Intercessors of the Lamb Religious

Community in Omaha, Nebraska, of which my son is a hermit. I frequently spoke about the Intercessors to my sister in our long phone conversations from Texas to Pennsylvania. At the time, we were both experiencing difficult times in our lives and our conversations encouraged one another. We spent many hours on the phone sharing our faith and praying together. It was then that she discovered that Mother Nadine, an Intercessor of the Lamb, was coming to Texas on mission. It was as if a door from heaven opened. After mother's talk, my sister noticed a table with material from *Direction for Our Times* and purchased the *Volumes*. When she began to read them, she experienced a joy that literally transcended through the phone waves. It was a spirit of joy that we both needed. Every day, she would say, "You must read these books, the *Volumes*."

I have found the "*Volumes*" to be the inspiration for changes taking place in my life in pursuing the "rescue mission for souls." The words in the *Volumes* stirred my faith in a way that renewed and refreshed my spirit, especially in my vocation as wife and mother. I had no doubt that it was Jesus speaking these words, spurring on this conversion of heart I was experiencing. It was an "Epiphany" a manifestation of a fresh spiritual renewal. It was there all the time, I just needed to be reminded of what laid dormant within. We need this heavenly sustenance as we move from the Age of Disobedience to the Age of Obedience. Change is difficult, and we are now in a time of transition.

Since the *Volumes*, my sister and I have initiated lay apostles Prayer Groups in our own parishes. The stories among our fellow lay apostles have renewed our spirits and deepened our love for God. When at a conference in Omaha with the Intercessors of the Lamb, one of the priests speaking said, "I bet each of you get up every morning and say, Lord, I have come to serve you today... give me something I don't want to do!" Of course the crowd roared with laughter knowing that we would never say such a prayer. However, it was an eye-opening statement. Since then I have shared this eye-opening prayer with our lay apostle Prayer Group and before we leave our meeting, we put on a big smile and say, "Lord, I have come to serve you today... give me something I don't want to do! Try it sometime. You will find that you are serving the Lord in every capacity throughout the day, beginning with putting your feet on the ground when you get out of bed.

Natalia C., FL

I was given the book, *Climbing the Mountain* by a dear friend for my birthday more than 2 years ago. At first, when I started reading it, I thought how nice it was for someone to achieve holiness following what Jesus wants us to do. But I could never commit to this. I am too weak and lacking any kind of calling to achieve holiness. Well, I continued reading the book. More and more I realized that Jesus was calling me, loving me and wanting me to be part of this great mission. Halfway through the book I asked my friend about the *Volumes*. The next day she gave me all the *Volumes* as a gift. This was a sign from Jesus that He needed me to transform my heart and in some way get involved. He made everything so readily available to me. At that moment in my life and even now, I've gone through very difficult times that only my close family and He know.

God knows very well the timing of when to come knocking at our door to see if we'll let Him in. I thank the Holy Spirit for enlightening me by opening my heart and letting Him in at this point in my life and not waiting any longer. He used the messages through Anne to achieve this. Through the hundreds or thousands of messages from Jesus, Mary and the saints in the *Volumes*, my heart has been transformed. I have understood the importance of the Sacraments which before I practiced as something optional. Today I feel the spiritual and physical need to receive the Sacraments. This alone has given me the strength and peace I need in these difficult times in my life as well as assisting me in the responsibility of rearing three small boys in their spiritual health as they grow up into teens and adults. In my hometown, of Miami, I have since joined a lay apostle group, which includes the friend that gave me *Climbing the Mountain* and the *Volumes*. I thank the Lord for putting in her heart that great birthday gift. It became the 'birthday' of my new spiritual life.

Agnes R., Philippines

I have started using my own money for a monthly feeding in our hacienda for children and the elderly. Also, I am more patient and gentle with my husband because I pray to Jesus for help. I have stopped being so vain and materialistic especially after reading *Climbing the Mountain,* where Anne went to heaven.

> *There is no substitute that will grant the security offered by the family of God."*
> ~Climbing the Mountain, page 33, Blessed Mother

PART FIVE

Returning to the Sacraments

Holy Eucharist

Reconciliation

The Holy Eucharist

Such holiness is available to souls who visit and venerate Me in the Eucharist. I am the cure for every ill. I am the calm for every storm. I am the comfort for every sorrow.
~Volume Two, August 18, 2003, Jesus

Look into your life and begin by making a decision to adore Jesus in the Eucharist.
~Volume Seven, July 28, 2004, St. Thomas Aquinas

The Sacrament of the Holy Eucharist is my daily bread. Without it, the world would spin out of focus. The Body and Blood of Our Lord Jesus Christ gives me hope. Hope that I can achieve. Hope that I can become holier. Hope that, with Him, I can withstand any amount of pain and suffering.~Bonnie

Juli H.

I was given the beautiful gift of cancer that brought me back to Christ and ALL the Sacraments. In three short years, I went from random Mass and Eucharist to bi-weekly Mass, weekly Adoration & Confession.

Maria C-H.

I have been a 'reverted' Catholic due to modern day apparitions of the Blessed Virgin Mary occurring on a worldwide basis in the 1980's. I'm a cradle Catholic and have always gone to Mass. But, in ignorance of my faith, I disagreed with some areas of Catholic Doctrine. Upon my return to my faith through the Blessed Mother, she led me straight to her son,

231

Jesus in the Holy Eucharist. I immediately educated myself on all areas of Catholic belief. It was a matter of fully understanding the doctrines of my faith and once I understood the Church's stance on birth control, etc., I fully embraced my faith. I wrote some books to share my own newfound knowledge, and coasted through the next ten years.

The Volumes came into my hands a few years ago, by Divine Providence, through a friend. I quickly found other mothers in my parish privately reading these works, and we formed a group to discuss them and pray together.

The biggest change occurring as a result of reading all of Anne's books was a great urge to visit Jesus in Eucharistic Adoration daily, as I had already been doing a holy hour each week for many years.

While I was in Adoration, I felt Jesus also wanted me to receive and be with Him in the Holy Sacrifice of the Mass on a daily basis. I knew it in my heart, but didn't want to give up those extra minutes of sleep each morning. I told Jesus, "OK, I get it. I'll try." I never looked back, and have been attending daily Mass ever since; even through the *Volumes*, I felt Jesus calling me.

Teresa R., TX

I had my big lifetime, "conversion confession" about ten years ago, and was already on my road to conversion as an adult Catholic. However, as a result of attending the Eucharistic Day of Renewal, I was inspired to start an apologetics group with my husband and other couples. During that time we studied the Eucharist. In combination with the books: *Climbing the Mountain* and *Mist of Mercy,* I looked at the Eucharist totally differently than what my upbringing was.

I had an internal realization this was the body, blood, soul and divinity of Jesus. Whereas before I believed, but after reading Anne's books and *Volumes*, I really, really believed!

Holy Eucharist: Adoration Of The Blessed Sacrament

Come to Me in the Sacrament of the Eucharist and I will teach you about obedience, revealing its beauty and the strength that lies with this misunderstood virtue.
~Volume Two, August 26, 2003, Jesus

Also, Adoration of your Jesus in the Blessed Sacrament will give you an unlimited flow of graces which will grant you peace and guidance.
~Volume Nine, August 23, 2004, Jesus

Cristina, NY

About ten years ago when I was single, I always thought it was good to go to Adoration, because of my Catholic belief. But I didn't appreciate it as much as I do now. I had stopped going to Adoration because I was so caught up in the world. In reading the *Volumes*, I know that Jesus wants me to go to Adoration always. So, I started going again, but I didn't feel the closeness to Jesus right away: it took months. I kept my faith going because of His messages in the *Volumes*. I would go to Adoration and say, "Lord, I don't know why I can't seem to get it. I know you want me to come here, but I just don't feel you. I'm scared because I want to be the beacon of your word." One day after a few months, I woke up and went to Adoration and had a profound joy of being there; then, I began having the urge to attend. The *Volumes* are where I actually learned to apply the teachings of Jesus. The more I read, the more I got to know Jesus and understand Him for who He is. This made it easier to communicate with Him when I tell Him everything, just like I converse with friends. I pour out to Him all my hurts and pains. I used to just pray a general prayer about what I was going through, which is not how I pray now. I tell Him how I'm feeling and what I'm doing. Now that I'm able to do that, I have started to hear Him and feel His guidance. There is an inner prompting telling me what to do. I follow the words of Jesus in the *Volumes* in which He says. ' talk to me, tell me about your pain' and I would practice this while in Adoration. Whenever I have dilemmas, I go to Adoration and converse with Jesus. This is where I began to understand what it is to have a close relationship with Him. When I look back, yes, I prayed, but I didn't have the relationship I now have with Him.

> *I am going to share My deepest secrets with you. I am going to remove the veil from the tabernacle as never before. I want you to know Me. I want you to know Me in My miraculous form of the consecrated host. I am the Bread of Life. Yes. And I am your Jesus, also. I was a humble Man, who walked your paths of difficulty, want, and hardship.*
> ~Volume Two, August 17, 2003, Jesus

Vanessa L.

Because of these messages, I am going to Holy Hour every week and sometimes twice a week. A miracle indeed! I am frequenting confession more than once a month as I see my sinfulness even more. I am praying my rosary with more joy and am more involved with the pro-life movement in my community. By His grace, God has been using my new boldness to share my heart with women considering abortion as they pull into the parking lot for their abortion or birth control.

Many babies have been saved. I contribute this change in my behavior to these heavenly messages as our precious Lord speaks to my heart through Anne. Praise you, Jesus!

Teresa R., TX

The most amazing thing about the mission is how I was able to attend the first Eucharistic Day of Renewal held in Dallas, TX, June 2006. The night before, I was very excited about attending. That day my daughter swallowed a penny. We took her to the hospital and she ended up spending the night. The doctors decided they needed to remove the penny that morning via endoscopy. It was successful. However, on the way home, my husband and I got into a bad argument. and I asked him if I could still go to the Eucharistic Day of Renewal. He was very upset and his answer was no. He was very stressed out at the time. Instead of arguing with him as I normally would, I just said Lord if you want me to go, you'll get me there. We got home late in the morning, and I had already missed the first portion of the retreat. My daughter was fine and was able to eat eggs and then took a little nap. During her nap, I asked my husband again if I could go to the retreat and he said, yes, so I was very happy. I went out to start my car and I realized my keys were on my dresser in my room. My daughter was taking a nap in my room, so I had to go in there very quietly. I got my keys and went back out to my car and I had forgotten something else in my room so I had to go back in. I went in quietly, retrieved what I needed and went back out again. Well, I had to go back into my room a third time. My daughter woke up and her eyes were wide open. She said, mommy, I want to go with you. First of all, I was stunned she knew I was going anywhere since she was only three. Second of all, why would she want to go with me? I was very reluctant and told her she was going to stay home with her dad and go to the park and have fun. She said again, very seriously, mommy, I want to go with you. Instead of arguing I thought, "OK Lord," you must want her to go with me. I picked her up, took her in the car, and she went to the retreat with me. I was very nervous about her being wild because I knew that the portion of the retreat I was going to be at had a speaker and Eucharistic Adoration. I really wanted to be able to enjoy it and I guess I was being selfish. So I said, Lord I leave it up to you, if she is supposed to be here with me; help me make the best of it. I was able to listen to the speaker while my daughter was very well behaved and during Adoration, she fell asleep in my arms. Being able to hold her in my arms for the entire Adoration was extremely powerful and I recall telling my friends the next day how incredible the Adoration was. It was one of the most powerful Adorations I ever attended.

Children, come and sit with Me in the Sacrament of the Eucharist. I am in every tabernacle throughout the world. Think of one now, and picture Me there. Do I have a television? A radio? Of course not. Yet I am truly there.
~Volume Two, August 21, 2003, Jesus

Holy Eucharist: Holy Mass

Holy souls or souls working for Me, and this I hope is each one of you, should attend Mass as often as possible.
~Volume Nine, August 23, 2004, Jesus

When you attend Mass you are praying and worshipping with thousands of angels. Your guardian angel goes with you, of course, and is so grateful for the opportunity to rest in the heavenly companionship of his fellow angels.
~Volume Nine, August 24, 2004, Jesus

Norman L.

I am very grateful to have joined your group and receive your emails, especially your last email, which has reminded me to set my alarm to attend Sunday Church. Now I go every week, even though other things can get in the way and detour us from God. Everyone could use a calling every now and then.

Judy M., FL

My husband was a seasonal Catholic going to mass at Christmas and Easter. He hadn't been to confession since his confirmation. We've been married 20 years and I had been praying he would come back to the church, but he wasn't interested and thought he was doing enough on his own. When I got the Volumes I began reading one passage to him every night. He would really listen. He loved what they were saying. Before I knew it he willingly started coming to church on a regular basis. And, he looked forward to it. Within a short time, he was on fire. He went to a Cursillo which I prayed about for years. There, he had an encounter with the living Christ in the Eucharist, and he was on fire when he came back. This was someone uncomfortable with being outwardly Christian, but who began telling friends that weren't even Catholic, about his encounter!

It was such a blessing, and, he's been supportive of me along the way. Every few months, I have all the Lay Apostles, with their spouses, over for a social at my house. It's a great way to socialize with the group besides praying with them and to show their spouses that we are all normal human beings.

"All eyes on Christ, dear friends. With Him we cannot fail."
~Climbing the Mountain, pg. 7, Anne, a lay apostle

Reconciliation

Pray this prayer to Me and I will respond in mercy. Your soul will be washed clean. Little children of My Church on earth, you must not neglect the sacraments. Experience the sacramental graces of the confessional...
~Volume Three, December 20, 2003, God the Father

I also want to say that the Sacrament of Confession must be dusted off and rein-stituted.
~Volume 3, August 9, 2003, Blessed Mother

Testimony sent in unsigned:

My husband went to Confession after more than 20 years. Praise be to God!

Catherine B., MI

I hadn't gone to Confession in 30 years, and now I am going faithfully. It is a very good healing process.

Edward G.

I was a lukewarm Catholic. But, since pledging to recite the allegiance prayer of *DFOT*, I have joined a prayer group at my parish, Christ's Catholic Community, and am attending the Sacraments more frequently, especially Reconciliation.

"Some people think they do not want to go to Confession and confess their past sins because it means they are making a commitment to perfection. They think, 'I'm not ready to be perfect. I'm not

239

ready to change. I'm not ready to completely give up some of my bad habits or behaviors.' Please, please, please do not let this stop you from going to Confession. Jesus knows you will fail again. He accepts this."

~Mist of Mercy, page 50, Anne, a lay apostle

Author's Note

I'm an active dreamer. By that I mean, I have vivid dreams every night and remember most of them. Some stay with me upon rising causing me to ponder and to figure out their significance. One night after starting work on this book, a dream jolted me awake like no other. I was in a church with a few scattered people, praying. A strange noise coming from the back of the church distracted me. It sounded like feet scuffling across the floor. I turned around, and to my horror, two men with ski masks on, holding guns, were coming straight toward me. I scanned the church and saw none of the others. I stood up, shaking as they approached me. I asked what they wanted. A deep voice replied, "will you die for Him?" gesturing to the Crucifix. Without hesitation, I looked the man in the eyes and said, "absolutely." He pointed his gun at my forehead and fired. I felt the impact of the bullet penetrating my scalp, but felt no pain. I woke up, bolting out of my bed. Is my head bleeding? Am I really dead? I was disoriented until seeing my clock. Four-thirty am. Sitting on the edge of my bed after realizing it was a dream, I glanced at my sleeping husband, unaffected by my abrupt awakening. I was dripping with sweat. I got up, took a sip of water, changed my pajamas, and lay back down. Wide awake, I wondered what the dream signified.

I believe the dream was God's confirmation or reminder of commitment to Him and the apostolate of

Jesus Christ the Returning King. I had to be willing to die for Him, let alone, live in humility for Him. I was ready to commit living my life as a true lay apostle. I still have so much to learn. It took over 40 years to develop the aberrations in my personality; I know it will take time to remove them as well.

On my path to self-discovery, I have figured out the one basic human characteristic I lack...trust. Trust or lack thereof, fuels us to behave or react instinctively. In my case, trust was not easy to come by. My mother had a terribly traumatic childhood causing a lifetime of mental illness. Her deficiencies led to damaging personality traits. She was the queen of mistrust. In order to maintain control, she had to be the center of attention. As she matured, obsession with her own beauty and the attention she drew was used to manipulate those around her, especially men. My father fell quickly under her spell, marrying her six weeks after their first date. He pampered her fragile ego on a daily basis for as long as I can remember. Over time, it became exhausting for him. Mom was frequently hospitalized over the years for mental breakdowns. I read in my paternal grandmother's diary a few years ago that Mom was in the hospital for my 2nd birthday. My younger sister was only 5 months old. It must have been torture for her to be away from her babies. We were her sole purpose for living. I don't remember much about those days. What I do remember are the Electric Shock Therapy treatments, the deep depressions, the manic highs, the inappropriate behaviors, the suicide attempt, Dad's threats to leave and his humor to console us, her beauty, her strong Catholic faith, her devotion to the Blessed Mother and respect for the saints. Despite the drama, there was always love.

Through it all, I never blamed God. Not once. The mistakes I've made are rooted in my search for the Truth, my search for someone I could trust. Never did it occur to me that someone was God. After weathering promiscuity in high school, abortion, divorce from a 16 year marriage, single parenthood, remarriage, end of life care for both parents, and surviving empty nest syndrome, I've learned a few things...tolerance, acceptance, the power of prayer and forgiveness.

But the greatest gift God has given me, aside from my daughters, is trust. I lean on Him now. I trust any outcome to be His will. Don't get me wrong, the devil is working hard to destroy my newfound trust. The difference is I'm acutely aware of what is from God and what is from the evil one. This awareness led me to search for others who were hurting and now healed from this rescue mission. I share my story to assist others in their search for Truth.

Acknowledgements

First and foremost, I thank Jesus Christ, our Returning King for opening my eyes to His love and compassion.

To Anne, whose "yes" to our Savior changes lives, teaching us about all the love and support Jesus and Heaven have to give.

To Jim Gilboy – for having faith in me and my book. You are one of the kindest men on the face of this earth.

To my husband Steve, for his support and encouragement to follow my dreams of becoming a writer.

To my daughters, Mallorie, Whitney and Taylor. I could never have become who I am without the three of you. You are proof that I must have done something right to deserve such amazing daughters. You are my life, my joy and my heart. The Kevin's are just icing on the cake.

To my sister Sheryl and her daughters Hayley and Maddy – your miraculous conversions happened right before my eyes. Because of the three of you, I am infused with joy and love.

To my dear friends, Joyce and Paul for introducing me to this apostolate and supporting my faith journey, loving me through it all.

To Karen and Kathleen, my sister lay apostles. Your faith is inspiring more than you know. You were heaven sent to provide the calm and love I so desperately needed in friends.

To Father Darragh for answering an email from an unknown writer. I am honored to know you.

To Jane Gomulka for turning an article idea into a book. Your energy and love are magnetic.

To Jane Miller for facilitating the writing of this book and keeping me in check with reality. Your dedication to this apostolate is magnificent.

To Steve Logan for making sure all "t's" are crossed and "i's" dotted. Your kindness and support are appreciated more than you know.

To the *DFOT* staff in the US and Ireland – Crystal and Kevin, Larry, Barbara, Mary Ellen, Sheri, Mary Ita, Nora, and Claire. You all are shining examples of what a Christian should be.

To Karen Anne, Emma, Keith, Ryan, Patrick, Tim, Kathleen, and Janie – the discerning young men and women dedicated to this apostolate and spreading God's love. You all have made it cool to be Catholic!

To all lay apostles, let's build this army together and unite.

Appendix

Children of Mexico - a mission providing multi-modes of communication to children who are disadvantaged and disabled to improve their quality of life. For more information or volunteer opportunities contact: Margarita Fajardo, MS, CCC-SLP, 524 Hemlock Ave, S. San Francisco, CA 94080; Phone: 650-784-6092; Fax: 650-583-6092; Email: childrenofmex@gmail.com

Enthronement of the Sacred Heart - The Sacred Heart Apostolate, Inc. is a global movement for creating a civilization of love through the Enthronement to renew societies by centering families on the Love of God incarnated in the Heart of Christ and founded by Fr. Mateo Crawley-Boevey sscc in Paray-le-Monial, France in 1907. It was endorsed by the Catholic Church as a global movement which continues to renew families in every continent. For more information contact: Gloria Anson, Sacred Heart Apostolate, Inc., 417 South Orchard Road, Syracuse, NY 13219; Phone: 800-851-5320; Fax: 315-492-3407; Email: sacredhc@verizon.net

Rosary Congress - Greater New Orleans Rosary Congress- "for life, reparation and peace in our city, nation and the world." Annual event. Contact: Marie at 504-508-7100 or visit the website:www.rosarycongress.org

Note from Maria P., NY (tragedy section): If you'd like more information about my son, Dominik or you just like to get to know him you may visit his website: www.dominik-pinzone.memory-of.com

Queen of Peace Center, Dallas, TX - a non-profit, tax-exempt organization founded to help promote and distribute information regarding the apparitions of Our Lady in Medjugorje, Bosnia-Hereegovina. For further information, contact Eleanor Wetzel at 214-368-1966.

Gift of Peace by John T. Mudd - www.prayforpeace.com
Note from John's mother, Ann: My son John, tragically died in a house fire just before Christmas. He left behind very little. However, he had just written a book of prayers for peace that seemed to bring our family much comfort. It is quite an irony that our pain would be eased by his own words. In an effort to spread that comfort around today, we are launching a website that tells a little about him as well as a way to get the Gift of Peace prayer book. You will also notice on one of the links to Medjugorge Magazine there is the story of both deaths of my children, Tricia and John. It was a great honor for this story to be published. My hope in sending you this website is not that you will purchase the book, but that you might help spread the word. Continuing John's work is now my mission.